Casting for Sculptors

The author at home. Photograph by Eric Thorburn

Casting for Sculptors

Vincent F. Butler

A & C Black · London

First published in Great Britain 1997
A & C Black (Publishers) Limited
35 Bedford Row
London WC1R 4JH

ISBN 0-7136-4525-3

A CIP record for this title is available from the British Library.

Cover illustrations:
Front: The Author in his studio

Back: Figure by the Author

Design by Alan Hamp

Typeset in 10/13pt Meridien by SPAN Graphics Ltd, Lingfield, Surrey
Printed and bound in Great Britain by Butler and Tanner Ltd, Frome and London

Contents

Introduction　　　　　　　　　　　　　　　　　7

Aims of this book　　　　　　　　　　　　　　9

1 · Casting by the waste mould method　　11

2 · Reproduction moulding　　　　　　　　27

3 · Modelling directly in plaster or cement　38

4 · Casting in cement　　　　　　　　　　41

5 · Casting in glass fibre reinforced resin　43

6 · Bronze casting by the lost wax process　45

7 · Casting by the ceramic shell method　64

8 · Modelling in clay　　　　　　　　　　65

9 · General information about casting
　　　metals for sculpture　　　　　　　　73

10 · George Mancini, bronze caster par
　　　excellence　　　　　　　　　　　　75

11 · Tools　　　　　　　　　　　　　　　79

12 · The making of 'Heritage and Hope',
　　　a large bronze casting　　　　　　　81

List of suppliers　　　　　　　　　　　　95

Index　　　　　　　　　　　　　　　　　96

Dedication
To my family

Introduction

This book is a collection of a lifetime's experience, both as a practising sculptor and as a tutor in one of Britain's major art schools, recording methods and techniques evolved over long years of practice and including a few which might no longer be widely in use, but which ought not to be lost in the mists of passing time.

I was always well aware in my years as a teacher how little time and effort was given to technical methods in sculpture schools. This was partly due to the brevity of the courses and to the ever widening range of materials being introduced into the curricula, but also to the undeniable fact that the greater emphasis was on the development of the idea alone, expressed more through construction methods than by modelling or even carving, so that casting was generally reduced to a short course of a mere day or two or even neglected altogether. In many art schools the craft aspects were often handed over entirely to technicians drawn from industry, who, however skilled they might have been in a particular direction, were not sculptors themselves and therefore could not know all the little tricks and nuances which artists build up in their repertoire as the years go by. This meant that generations of students graduated from art school with perhaps a little experience in welding metal or jointing wood, but with almost no knowledge of moulding and casting. Certainly those whose training in sculpture has been exclusively through evening or part-time classes would have no opportunity of learning how to cast their clay works and would either have to pay others to do the work for them or risk disasters by trying to tackle it themselves with only minimum skills and experience.

I would not however wish to give the impression that in the past things were somehow better, because they were not. In my eight years in three different art schools, I had to fight hard to persuade my tutors to show me how to make efficient moulds as they preferred to restrict their teaching to generalised so-called 'crits', which were usually verbose, mostly without substance and frequently incomprehensible and they were notably reluctant to roll up their sleeves and get their hands dirty.

In my student years in the 1950s, very few sculpture schools had their own foundries or even a kiln for firing terracotta and while the emphasis in those distant days was on modelling in clay, very little instruction was given in casting. Then it was the norm to model from life and then throw away the result in order to start afresh, putting off the casting until some unspecified future, which for many students actually meant never.

I cannot be sure what was the situation in other countries but my own years in the Fine Art Academy in Milan did little to extend my knowledge of craft, because although it was a famous art academy, staffed at that time by such major figures as Marini, Minguzzi and Messina, no instruction in moulding was given and there was not even a store of materials beyond a tubful of muddy clay, which in the wintertime was covered in ice, so cold was it in the high ceilinged, ill-lit studios on the ground floor of the National Gallery and Pinacoteca. Everything had to be brought in by the students themselves and I still recall falling off my bicycle in the Via Brera and seeing my 50 kilo bag of plaster, which I had balanced on the handlebar, disappear under the wheels of a passing tram!

This book then is an attempt to share a lifetime's experience as both a sculptor and as a teacher with students of sculpture – be they amateurs or full-time.

Finally, it would not be appropriate for me to produce this book without acknowledging the debt I owe to the late George Mancini, bronze caster par excellence, with whom I had the privilege of working for a brief few years after he closed down his foundry in Edinburgh and from whom I learnt so much of what I have recorded in these pages.

George Mancini and Vincent Butler in the foundry

Aims of this book

The aim of this book is principally to provide a description of the basic casting techniques that are essential for those sculptors, whether 'amateurs' or art school graduates, whose main interest is in making their images in clay, which has then to be converted into a permanent form, either in bronze, plaster, cement or resin.

The aim of this book is not to compete with other, similar publications on the same subject, but rather to complement them, in that its intention is to focus on those numerous little hints and methods of carrying out the often complex tasks involved in the moulding and casting of sculpture, many of which can appear to be out of the reach of the amateur or part-time sculptor. The author has therefore carefully avoided trying to give instruction in how to draw, model or carve, steering well clear of aesthetic or artistic guidance and concentrating entirely on the procedures needed to convert modelled images into a permanent form.

The text is directed principally at those courageous individuals who, while not having had the privilege of a full-time training at an art school, so love the craft of sculpture that they dedicate much energy and time to their work, but so often do not know how to cast it efficiently or cheaply and occasionally end up with disastrous results.

For this reason every effort has been made to concentrate on working methods that can be adopted by 'amateurs', who are likely to have only limited funds and little studio space available to them, but who wish to master at least the basic aspects of the craft.

Obviously the techniques of casting in bronze will not easily be within the grasp of the part-timer, and indeed very few professionals have their own personal foundries or even the skills required for metal casting. However, there are ways and means of preparing one's sculpture so as to reduce the amount of work and expense that otherwise has to be done by commercial foundries.

Moreover, since modern art schools have almost entirely abandoned figurative modelling in favour of abstract construction, almost no casting is being taught and so many techniques are therefore in danger of disappearing altogether, or of being substituted with more expensive or wasteful methods.

The author therefore hopes that this book will have something to say to those few students who have not entirely discarded modelling, or who might one day wish to return to it. The passion for creating modelled or carved images of the human figure in particular, which has been part of civilisation since the dawn of time, will not die a natural death and will continue to survive despite contemporary attempts to subdue it.

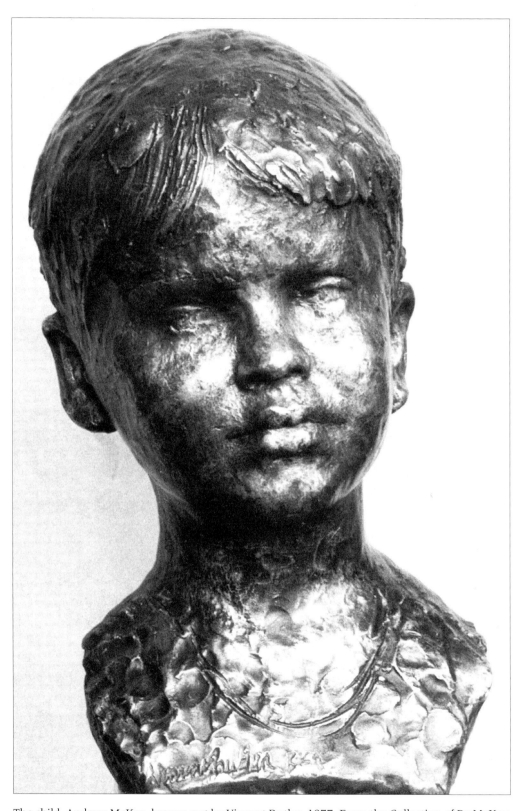

The child, Andrew McKay, bronze cast by Vincent Butler, 1977. From the Collection of Dr McKay

1 · Casting by the Waste Mould Method

This is the simplest and the most common of all moulding methods, and is fundamental to a wide range of casting operations. It is essentially a 'one off' process, in which the original image or model (normally being in clay) as well as the mould itself, is destroyed, so that we end up with a single replica of our original. This therefore is the method used for converting a non-permanent material, such as clay, into a permanent material such as plaster, cement, etc. The simplest example of such casting would be for a flat relief panel, using a one-piece mould. However, for the purposes of this book, we shall begin rather with a two-piece mould, and we shall take a head as our example.

The Mould

As in all casting, it is essential that the clay model should be soft, as it will need to 'give' as the mould is prised off. The first step is to decide on a suitable parting line or joint. In the case of a head, this should be drawn vertically behind the ears, so that the seam will not be visible when the finished cast is viewed from the front. We now prepare a clay wall or band, by flattening a sheet of stiffish clay and cutting it into strips about 1½in. wide by ¼in. thick (4cm x 6mm). These strips are then laid, edge on, along the seam line that we have already marked on the clay. The front edge of the band should be tight up against the surface; to hold it in place it is useful to place small lumps of clay behind it as supports. We have now divided the head into two 'halves', the front, being bigger than the back section, is referred to as the 'mother mould'.

We now mix a small basin of casting plaster into which we have stirred a spoonful of powder colour, so that the first layer of the mould will be coloured. This will provide us with a warning as we are later chipping away the mould to reveal the cast within. This mixture, which should not be too stiff, should be splashed evenly all over the face and up to the top edge of the clay wall. It should be left rough on its surface so that it binds well with the subsequent layers. Some moulders, at this point, put a few dabs of clay wash onto the surface to facilitate separation later. I personally do not do this, although I like to place small pieces of clay in the deep recesses, such as in the ears, behind the ear lobes, under heavy locks of hair etc., so that I thereby create weak spots in the mould at all deep parts where the cast is delicate and could be easily broken in the chipping out process. If the head you are casting has a neck, it is useful at this stage to lay on a couple of reinforcing bars of ½in. (12mm) mild steel, running from the temples to the shoulders. We complete the mould by smoothing a final layer of plaster all over and right up to the top edge of the seam band, making sure, as best we may, that we have not made some areas too thick and others too thin. Then we leave it to set.

When it is set, we take away the clay band, and using a knife, we trim away all rough edges. After this, we make a number of notches or shallow holes in the face of the seam (an old screwdriver filed to a 'v' shape is ideal for this), to act as registers for the second half of the mould. This wall should then be coated with a clay slip or soap or oil, as a separator. Clay slip is the best for this as it leaves a clear grey line in the mould.

We complete the mould by repeating the process on the rear half, i.e. first a coloured layer, then a final coat of normal plaster. We should be sure to scrape a knife all along the seam to ensure that one side has not overlapped onto the other.

Then we proceed to open the mould and prepare it for filling. If we wish, we may place the whole mould in a bath of water and leave it to soak for a while which will cause the clay to swell and the seams to start to open up. In the case of a heavy mould, it is normally sufficient

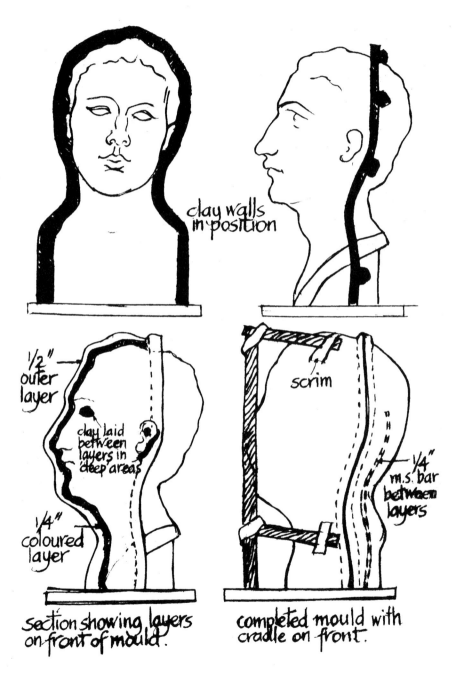

clay walls in position

1/2" outer layer

clay laid between layers in deep areas

1/4" coloured layer

section showing layers on front of mould.

scrim

1/4" m.s. bar between layers

completed mould with cradle on front.

Method of making a waste mould of a head in two pieces

to spray the surface with water and then to gently tap a knife blade into the seam until it starts to open. Then, with careful leverage, the smaller half of the mould will come away and may be put aside to await the next stage in the work. The mother mould will not pull away from the armature so it is necessary for us to dig out most of the clay from the inside.

Both parts of the mould should now be rinsed to remove any remaining traces of clay. If there are any air bubbles in the surface, we can simply press some clay into them and smooth carefully. The next task is to apply a separator to the surface. My favourite material for this is household detergent soap, brushed on twice, but other equally effective separators are soft soap, or soda solution, or shellac and wax.

For filling, I generally lay the two halves on the bench and coat them with approximately a ½in. (12mm) of fresh plaster, paying attention to the deep places. (Note that the mould should not have been allowed to dry out before filling.) Just before this first layer has set, I normally insert small brass pins into such deep areas as the ear lobes to act as reinforcements. We now place the two halves of the mould together locking them with 'dogs'. These are simple clamps made by bending 6in. (15cm) nails into a 'goal post' form and sharpening the ends. They are then gently hammered into the mould, bridging the seams. Some moulders prefer to place small pieces of scrim soaked in plaster across the seams, but I prefer to use dogs as they force the edges of the seam hard together.

We now must prepare another bowl of plaster and pour it into the open mould, rolling it around to coat the inside up to about 1in. (2.5cm) in thickness. In the case of a head with a long neck, we might insert a reinforcing bar at this stage. This might stop at the edge of the mould or alternatively can be left protruding to give an anchor point for fixing the cast onto a plaster block later.

As soon as the plaster is set, which is almost immediately, we may continue to the chipping out stage. This is done with a small flat chisel whose corners have been rounded off, and an ordinary hammer. Some people use a wooden mallet for this work, but I find a hammer is better as it delivers a sharp, decisive blow with little force. It is important to adopt a strategy in chipping out a cast, as random working will only lead to confusion. Therefore, I recommend that we begin at the top and work down the seams, then across the forehead, leaving the eyes and ears to the last. These areas we will need to pick out with great caution. Our coloured layer, as it comes into view, will serve as a warning to us that we are nearing the surface of the cast.

Repairing Small Defects or Damage

It is almost inevitable that we will find the odd air bubble on the surface of our cast, or that we will chip into the plaster in one or two places. The best way to deal with such defects is to mix up a very small quantity of plaster with a lot of water, and then using a small paint brush, carefully fill the damage, smoothing out as we do so. The same watery mix will also serve as glue to fix any small bits that have broken off. Another method that I use a lot to fill holes, etc. on the surface of a cast is to brush the affected area with white shellac and press a small quantity of clay onto it, repeating until sufficient bulk is built up. The shellac will prevent the clay from shrinking and falling out and may be sanded smooth when dry. This method is effective also for adding small amounts of remodelling, if so desired, but of course it results in a rather messy appearance. This may, however, be disguised by colouring the cast altogether.

Variant Methods of Casting a Head

Some sculptors occasionally prefer to make use of brass shim as fencing for the seam on a mould, instead of clay wall. This has certain advantages where the mould is fairly small and the plaster may be applied to both sides of the wall at once. However, where we need more than one bowl of plaster, it is just as easy to

Chipping out a waste mould of a bust

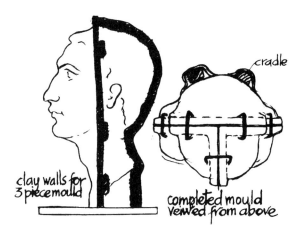

clay walls for 3 piece mould

cradle

completed mould viewed from above

Method of making a three-part waste mould of head

make a clay wall and do each half at a time. I personally dislike the brass shim method for the simple reason that, as I like to smooth my mould by hand, I find the shims can cause severe cuts to the fingers unless one is very cautious.

Three-part Waste Mould of a Head

Another method of moulding a head which I frequently use is to divide the mould into three sections, rather than two as described above. My reason for doing this is that, by so doing, I can remove the mould easily without destroying the clay, so that I can then, if I so desire, return to the sitter and continue to work the portrait, perhaps into a second version. The method of dividing into three is as follows: The front seam will now be along the hairline and down across the cheekbones and neck, and another seam will depart at right angles to this, over the skull and down the back of the neck. By this means the three parts of the mould come away very easily, leaving the original clay virtually undamaged. The disadvantages with this method are that the sections are more difficult to assemble, and there will, of course, be a visible seam on the face, but there are clear advantages as well, and we must make our choice.

Portrait of Christine Walker, bronze, modelled and cast by Vincent Butler, 1973. From the Walker Family Collection

Casting a Flat Panel or Relief

A flat relief or panel should always be modelled on a board that is strong enough to resist warping under the wet clay, and wide enough to be clamped or screwed down while casting, as it is extremely difficult to open a mould from a panel which moves about. Reliefs larger than say 20 in. (51cm) should be modelled vertically on a wall and the base board should be wide enough to leave plenty of room all round for the mould to rest on. We should always ensure that our relief is thick enough to allow for metal reinforcing to be placed in the cast, as it is so easy to miscalculate depth and leave us with too thin a cast. With large reliefs we must also be careful to slightly chamfer the edges so that our mould pulls off without resistance; we must not allow the clay to come away with the mould as its sheer weight could easily break the plaster.

The method of moulding a relief is as before, using a coloured layer followed by a normal layer of plaster, and paying great attention to the thickness. One of the biggest problems with flat forms is their tendency to warp and twist. To avoid this the mould must be well reinforced with metal bars, and in the case of moulds larger than say 20 in. (51cm), we should also add a cradle. This is simply made of wooden cross bars attached to the surface of the mould by short lengths of scrim soaked in plaster. When the mould is turned over it will rest safely on this support. Where the panel has been modelled vertically on a wall, these wooden posts can be extended down to ground level in such a way that, as the mould is eased off the clay, they act as legs and carry the weight of the mould until we are able to rest it on the work bench, after which we saw them off.

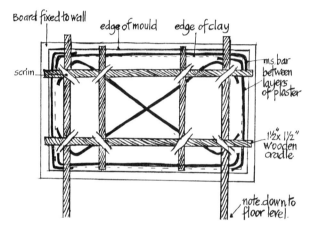

Elevation showing minimum reinforcements

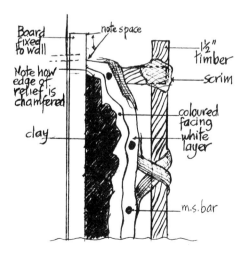

Method of moulding a relief panel on a wall

Fine Details

In the case of a panel with high relief where the mould might not pull away from the clay so easily, it is often good practice to mould the high projections separately, removing the sections and thereby reducing the panel to a flat background. These can then be cast apart and attached to the main panel later. A favourite little trick of mine, when I have had to cast a very high relief and then found that moulding and chipping out small details has resulted in breaking tiny hands and feet, etc., has been simply to sever the details from the background, dry them out and fire them in the kiln to biscuit temperature, making sure that I have added a small projection of clay to serve as an anchor. After casting the panel into plaster, it is a simple matter to attach the fired details. Of course, it will then be necessary to disguise the difference in colour by staining the whole panel.

15

'The Woman Taken in Adultery', relief for St Mary's Camelon, Falkirk, done by Vincent Butler, 1981, plaster, 8' x 2'.

As an alternative to this, where for example, a kiln might not be easily available, I have developed another strategy for casting small details which avoids the problems of breakage encountered when using a waste mould. It is as follows: The detail to be cast is first severed from its background, then a nail or short wire is inserted into its stump to act as a grip, and the whole thing is lightly brushed with oil. We should now make up a saucepan of liquid modelling wax and gripping the detail by the wire, we dip it into the hot wax, several times over until it is coated up to about a ¼ in. (6mm) all over. We allow this to cool. Then, using a surgeon's scalpel, we cut through the wax along a line corresponding to the seam we would have in standard casting; we also cut around the nail. All we need to do now is to soak the whole thing in water for a short time and the mould will come away in two halves. These must be carefully washed to remove all traces of clay and oil, and then the two halves can be joined together again, using hot wax to seal the seam. We may then fill the mould with plaster, inserting a short length of reinforcing wire if we so desire. As soon as the plaster has set, we simply place the whole mould in a pan of hot water and in a short time the wax will melt,

float to the surface and leave our cast, clean and whole at the bottom. We can then proceed to attach it to the appropriate place on the panel.

The two methods of casting fine details described above are simple and effective ways of avoiding the almost guaranteed damage which occurs when you attempt to cast small objects by the standard waste mould method. I have described this strategy with reference to the casting of a relief panel. However, I myself use it in any cast where there are vulnerable areas, such as arms and legs where it is so difficult to avoid shattering fingers and toes by other methods. Obviously the limitation to this method is size, and we can only use this for objects that can be easily placed in a pan of hot water.

Filling a Relief Mould

Continuing from before, we may now proceed to fill the mould of our relief. The first thing to do is to apply a suitable separator, be it soap or soda, or, if we wish to follow a more traditional recipe, shellac and wax. Liquid plaster is then flooded into the mould, reinforcing bars are inserted and flat areas should be strengthened with jute scrim, well pressed into the plaster. The final task is to turn the mould over and carefully chip out, remembering always that as soon as the cast is released from its mould, it will have a tendency to warp, so we must be sure that our internal reinforcing bars are sufficiently strong to prevent this. On the question of reinforcing metals, it was traditional at one time to coat all such metals with a layer of pitch, paint or shellac, to avoid rusting, but I personally do not do this, as I find that small rust stains appearing on the surface do not cause me any loss of sleep.

Casting a Figure

In the case of a figure or any model more complex than a head, the same basic principles of casting will apply, but the mould will have more than two pieces and can easily have half a dozen or more. As previously described, there will be one main piece or 'mother mould', and numerous smaller sections. In a standing figure or other vertical form, the entire front will form the mother mould and the back will be divided up into as many parts as proves to be necessary.

Pulpit relief for St Mary's Camelon, Falkirk, done by Vincent Butler, 1985, fibreglass, 4' x 4'.

Where there are limbs that project out from the figure, it is sometimes useful to cast these separately, whereas if, for example, the arms run straight down the sides, it is often more convenient to cast them as part of the main mould, that is, half to the front and half to the back.

Having decided on the parting line, we proceed to lay a clay wall, or insert brass shims, all the way round and in between arms and legs. **Note:** In the case of a small figure, the space between limbs is often so small that it is not easy to insert a wall. What we might do instead is to shape a lump of clay to approximately fit the gap, oil it and push it in from the back until it completely fits the space. Once we have made the mould at the front, it will be a simple matter to slide out this clay plug and make the rear section of the mould up against the front. As we complete each part of the mould, we should remove the clay walls, remembering to make register marks on the seam faces and to apply clay wash to each such face, until the mould is complete. Any sections of the mould that are larger than about 6in. (15cm) should be reinforced with ¼in. (6mm) mild steel bar and in addition, the mother mould should have a wooden cradle.

In order to open the mould, it is possible to immerse it in water, if it is small enough, or otherwise to spray with water and then crack open the seams by inserting a knife blade and tapping gently. When the mould has been rinsed out, we should apply a separator and then proceed to fill. My normal practice has always been to use fine casting plaster for the mould and superfine for the cast. All thin or otherwise fragile parts of the cast should be reinforced with steel bar, bent and shaped to fit. This is specially important with a standing figure as the strain on the ankles will be too great unless there is adequate support inside them. As before, the chipping out process must be carried out carefully, first clearing the white layers and then, with even greater care, the final coloured surface coat.

Casting a Large Standing Figure

The method of casting a large work is the same as for a small piece, except that there will be more sections and a strong cradle will be required for the mother mould. Taking a full-sized standing figure as our example, the procedure is as follows: First lay our clay walls, about 2½in. (64mm) wide, along a parting line which is set, as seen from the front, just 'over the horizon', and which runs from the base on one side, up over the head and down to the base on the other side. At the top of the head I normally stop my wall just above the ears and then add another band in a circle around the crown, so that it will form a cap which is the first piece to be removed and the last to be replaced during filling. Where there are arms, I normally do not include these in the mould as split sections, but contain them entirely in the mother mould and provide them with up to three 'caps'. This is because it would be very difficult to pull off the back sections *including* the arms.

The next thing to do is to prepare a quantity of coloured plaster and apply it all over the front of the figure, up to the edges of the walls. On top of this we should add plenty of mild steel reinforcing bars which have been bent to follow the contours of the figure. We then complete the front section with 1in. (2.5cm) thick white plaster, smoothing out as we go along. Finally, we add a stout cradle of 2in. (5cm) by 1in. (2.5cm) wooden spars running from just above the head to the base at its lower edge. There will be two main vertical spars, and several cross bars, all tied in firmly with short lengths of scrim soaked in plaster and pressed firmly into place. Remember that this cradle will have to carry the entire weight of the mould and cast, right up to the chipping out stage, so it must be strong, and well and truly fixed to the mould with scrim.

Our next task is to remove the clay walls, provide register holes at intervals of about 4in. (10cm) and coat the seams with clay wash. Now we must proceed to divide up the rear section of the figure into as many pieces as we need, by placing clay walls horizontally across the figure, from seam to seam. In the case of a life-sized figure, these will probably occur at the back of the knees, just below the buttocks, at the point where the rear supporting armature enters the figure, below the shoulder blades and finally at the aforementioned skull cap level. The determining factor in deciding where to put our seams is quite clearly the distance we are able to reach with our arms when we come to fill up the mould. Therefore no section should be longer than a forearm. We start at the bottom and work our way up, removing each clay wall in turn and clay washing each new seam.

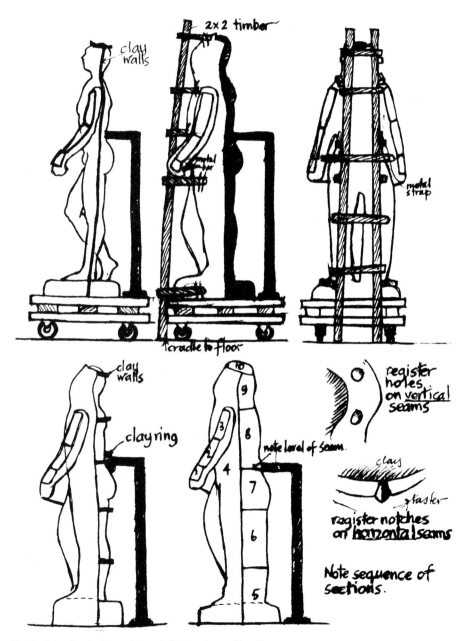

Typical method of moulding full-sized standing figure

Standing nude, life-sized bronze by Vincent Butler, 1984. Cast by Art Bronze Foundry, Fulham. From the collections of Finkbeiner, Garmisch Partenkirchen; Wilke, Wolfsburg and Franceschi, Milan. Photograph by Andrew Purvis

Register holes in these sections will not be drilled directly down into the seams this time, but will be notches cut into the edge, as vertical registers would break away as each section is pulled off later. Do not forget to add strong reinforcement bars to each piece as you go along, and keep the seams scraped clean, so that you do not lose sight of the parting line. I normally leave a small wedge of clay in the seam at intervals, so that I have a clearly marked place to insert a chisel, later, when I come to open the mould in preparation for filling.

Note: I have occasionally observed students using scrim in a mould, having been told to do so by ignorant tutors. This is quite wrong as scrim will make the work of chipping out very difficult. However, it is common practice among professional moulders to lay long twists of scrim along each seam. The purpose of this is to make the seam stronger and less likely to break when dogs are knocked in, or when tools are inserted to force the sections apart. However, such scrim should never be allowed to spread over the surface of the mould. Personally, I do not use any scrim as I always wish to economise on costs, but there is a risk of breakage at the edges with unscrimmed plaster.

As soon as the mould is completed, we must proceed with the task of removing the rear sections. Beginning at the top, it is usually quite easy to prise off the top cap first of all. This will allow us to dig out the clay from the head, and then to fill up the space with water which will slowly seep down the entire mould. Soon, with care and attention, we will be able to free the other sections, right down to the base at the back. For the front, we have to dig out the clay until it becomes possible to walk the whole mother mould off the armature and lay it horizontally on its cradle. All parts should be carefully cleaned and a good separator applied.

The next job is to prepare strong reinforcing irons, and great care must be taken with these to bend them to fit the contours. They should run from the top of the head down to the feet and be right-angled into the base. For a large work which we might wish to exhibit as an uncoloured plaster, it would be advisable to paint the irons with rust inhibiting paint. Some moulders wrap wire around each one to give greater grip against the plaster. The irons are fixed into the mother mould by means of blobs of plaster. When they are firmly in place, we may pull the mould upright again and begin filling. My personal preference at this point is to fit the rear base section in place before turning the mould upright, simply so that I can get access to the base from below and fill it level.

Having filled the base, we now attach the next piece, knock in our dog clamps and pour plaster down into the space. This is repeated for the next piece up to the top of the thighs. From here on it is good practice to make the cast hollow, by applying the plaster by hand to the vertical surfaces. The layer can be up to about 2in. (5cm) thick.

We continue in this way until we reach the shoulders. We will see that it will probably be impossible to get a hand down into the shoulder section at this point, so what we have to do is to line the section first then place wet plaster all along the adjacent seams and press it quickly into its position, hammering dogs into the seams to force them to close up tight. This is always a tricky thing to do and we will almost certainly find that we have some gaps to fill up from the outside of the cast. We have now almost filled the entire mould. The body is hollow and we should have also lined the head section, up to the crown. My habit here is to stuff the head with newspaper, rather than fill it solid, seal it off with a little plaster and put the crown section onto it. I have already drilled a small hole right at the highest point of the crown and through this I now pour plaster which fills the top of the head completely.

Chipping out may begin as soon as the plaster has set. Start by chipping along the seams and gradually working across each piece until the whole figure is freed. Where we have tied the cradle with scrim, we should cut through the fixing with a saw rather than attempt to break through with the chisel. If, whilst we are removing the mould, we come across small areas of the cast that we see have not filled up completely, we should do whatever we can to fill them at once while there is still at least part of the mould to guide us. Any surface holes or damage caused during the chipping out may be filled afterwards in the way I have described on page 13. A life-sized figure might well require two or three days to chip out completely. Do not rush it or you will certainly do damage to the surface.

Susanna, life-sized bronze by Vincent Butler, 1982. Cast by Art Bronze Foundry, Fulham

Casting a Sitting or Reclining Figure

The method of casting figures other than standing is no different in principle, except that perhaps it will not be so obvious where the mother mould will be. In practice, if we start off by making a cap right down the back of our figure, making sure that it will pull away easily, then we can simply regard all the rest of the mould as the 'mother'. It will, of course, have caps on all its limbs, which will pull off, allowing us access to clean out the clay. There will be as many caps as we need, according to how big the figure is, to enable us to reach all parts for cleaning and for fixing our reinforcing irons into place. On small figures we might only need irons through the neck, arms and legs, but a full-sized work will require a substantial inner skeleton of metal, just as we saw in the case of the standing figure.

When dealing with small works it is often difficult to make the mould light enough on parts such as arms, to render chipping out easy, and we often break them beyond repair. If you refer to page 15 you will see I describe a method of severing these small details and casting them apart, to be added later.

At this point it might be worth mentioning a method I used extensively at one time for the casting of small works which resulted in my making a very thin and light mould that chipped off the cast with no difficulty whatsoever. I no longer use it but it perhaps ought to be recorded. I would take a strong cotton thread and lay it along the seam of my figure, gently pressing it into the surface of the clay so that it could not fall off. Then, making up a small amount of plaster, I would cover the thread completely with a band about ½in. (12mm) in width. Just as this was starting to set, I would carefully pull the thread away, cutting through the plaster and thereby making the division. I would repeat this for all seams and then simply fill in the spaces between, adding reinforcing wire where necessary. You will see that you have to be nimble fingered with this method but it does give you a mould that is paper thin. Of course, it is not possible to have a coloured layer with such a mould and it cannot be used for big moulds, but it has some interesting aspects and could be worth trying.

Designing the Seams of a Mould

One problem I have frequently encountered when advising students about mould making was that they often could not even begin to think where to place their seams. There is no set formula for the design of a mould, and wherever you make your seams you will almost certainly find that the mould will open easily enough. However, it should be borne in mind that there are a few things to think about in planning a seam.

1. Every mould should have a main section or 'mother mould' against which all the smaller sections are fitted.
2. All minor sections or caps should be long enough for you to extract the clay through them and insert reinforcing irons, as well as pour in your required casting materials – this will differ slightly between plaster, cement, resin or wax, for example.
3. Where there are parts of the figure so inaccessible that you could end up with your mould being too thin or too thick in places, it might be better to sever the part in question, cast it apart and attach it afterwards.

I occasionally noted that a student would make a set of caps on a mould and then block them off by attaching the cradle over them, preventing access to them. If it proves difficult to place a cradle on a mould without interfering with the caps, then it might be that the only thing to do is to open the cap and clear out the clay inside it, *before* putting the cradle on. This will still leave the difficulty of filling afterwards but often enough access can be found in another place.

Designing a Mould of a Four-legged Animal

Moulding animal figures ought not to be more difficult than moulding any other kind of figure, but we will normally have at least three legs connected to the base as well as the central supporting iron, all of which requires a certain care if we are to avoid making it difficult to pull the halves of the mould apart. Therefore, the parting line along the base must be carefully planned to enable the mould to separate easily without locking. This base line will conform to one of three possible patterns as shown in the illustration below.

Having decided which pattern best suits our particular case, we place shims or a clay wall along the dividing line, rising up each leg, across the underside and over the back, neck and head. If we are able to include the supporting iron in this line then well and good, otherwise we shall have to encircle it with clay to create a slot in the mould at that point. In the case of an animal with one hoof raised, the best way to deal with that is simply to cap it off, or alternatively, sever it completely and cast apart. Apply the same reasoning to the tail. If the animal's head is turned to one side, as well might be the case, then we should be careful to place our seam in such a way as to keep well clear of the eye.

We now proceed with a layer of coloured plaster, well reinforced with metals, and then our final coat of white plaster, following the previously described practice of treating each seam with clay wash and adding register notches, etc. Be very careful to avoid piling up thick quantities of plaster on the base, or you will have great difficulty in chipping out the relatively thin ankles and legs. If your animal is bigger than about 12in. (30cm), I would advise that you put a cradle on the 'main' side of the mould.

When your mould is complete, simply continue as in all casts, by opening the mould, cleaning it and adding a suitable separator, inserting adequate reinforcing irons and filling with fresh superfine plaster. This process should always be done with care and I think the best way in this case is to lock the entire mould together with dogs and pour the casting plaster down through one of the legs, allowing the air to escape from the others, until the mould is completely filled up. If you wish to make a hollow cast, then you will need to have a cap on the back of the animal, filling the mould in its natural upright position, so that the legs fill solid. Then, if you can reach inside, you can line the body parts by hand. This is the only possible method with an animal so large that it is not practical to turn the mould upside down.

Casting a Large Four-legged Animal

The method required for moulding a large-scale animal does not differ from that for a small work, except that we do not attempt to turn the

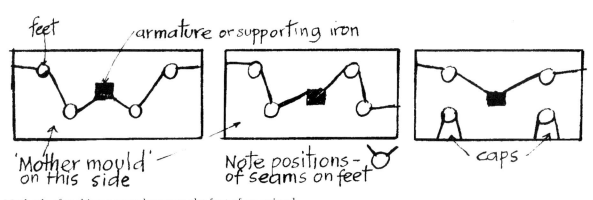

Methods of making a seam between the feet of an animal

mould upside down for filling. Instead, we will need additional mould sections or caps along the spine. These will give us the necessary access for filling the mould and they will also reduce the size and weight of the sections on the flanks. A good cradle will, of course, be vital for such a mould. Possible locations for top caps are shown below.

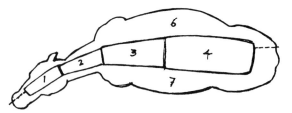

Probable location for spine caps on large mould

Rooster, bronze, 15" high, modelled and cast by Vincent Butler, 1975

Casting a Small-scale Animal

If your intention is to make an animal on a small scale, not larger than perhaps 6in. (15cm), I would suggest either modelling it in clay and firing it, or modelling it in solid wax and having it cast into bronze, or making a waste mould in plaster and filling it, not with plaster, but with resin – solid, without glass fibre, but inserting wires into the legs, etc.

Separators and Release Agents

These are barriers applied to the surface of a mould which seal the porosity and prevent the cast from sticking to the mould. We have already mentioned detergent soap or soda solution as good separators for plaster, and in this case they act as combined separator/release agent. An alternative for plaster casts is to apply shellac as a separator to the partly dried mould – probably three coats – and then apply a light coat of liquid wax polish as release agent. In this case it will be advisable to dampen the mould again before filling, in order to avoid suction from a dry mould.

Other separators for various casts are as follows:

> Cement casts from plaster moulds:
> Shellac and wax
> Wax casts from plaster moulds:
> Plain water
> Wax casts from gelatine moulds:
> Light oil applied sparingly
> Wax casts from rubber moulds:
> Normally no separator needed
> Plaster or cement casts from rubber moulds:
> Light wax polish
> Resin casts from plaster moulds:
> Follow manufacturer's advice, although I have found that shellac/wax or wax alone works well.

Note: the above recipes refer to the making of casts from moulds, but we also require separators sometimes when making the mould from an original model or pattern, and these will be as follows:

Gelatine moulds off plaster model:
Shellac and oil
Hot melt rubber moulds off plaster model:
No separator but dampen model to avoid air bubbles created by the heat
Cold setting rubber moulds off plaster model:
Shellac and wax or follow manufacturer's recommendations.

Using Plaster

As plaster is used in so many of our operations as sculptors, it is worthwhile mentioning methods of using it. I often found in my dealings with students that they would not mix their plaster correctly and such a simple error could sometimes lead to weak or broken moulds or casts.

Estimate the amount of plaster you will need with care. It is easy to make more than you can handle, resulting in waste. Sift the dry plaster into the water, quite quickly, but do not stir or agitate, until you have approximately as much plaster as water. Leave to stand until no more air bubbles arise. If you now have excess water on top of your mix, carefully pour it off (not down the sink or you will block your drain!). Do not add any more plaster. Then stir well and use. For first coats you use your mix at once while it is still liquid and therefore splashes well into the details on the surface of your model. Subsequent layers are applied when the plaster has stiffened to the consistency of thick cream so that each handful stays in place. When observing certain students at work I often wondered if they were casting their model or their own feet, as so much plaster simply fell off the mould! Others tried to avoid this by making their mixture so stiff, by adding far too much plaster to the water, that it had the consistency of porridge, resulting in a rock hard mould. As I mentioned earlier, I always use fine casting plaster for moulds and superfine for the cast.

Fine and superfine may be mixed together in any proportion as the setting time for each is the same. Some manufacturers produce specialist plasters, such as Dental or Herculite, etc., but I never found these to be any better than superfine which is so much cheaper. **Note**: if for any reason you wish to slow down the setting time of casting plaster, you may add a small quantity of glue size to your water. This also hardens the plaster slightly. Equally, if you wish to speed up your setting, then use slightly tepid water but, in general, modern plasters need no additives.

Colouring Plaster Casts

Sometimes it is desirable to treat plaster casts to make them attractive for exhibition, or simply to tone down the dead whiteness of plaster. There are various ways to do this, some of which are as follows:

1. Coat the dry plaster with a thin mix of wax polish and turps, into which you have stirred a small amount of black or brown artist's oil paint. Allow to dry and then wipe all over with a cloth dampened with turps so as to tone the general effect with a subtle shade. Allow to dry thoroughly then lightly polish. The effect will be ivory-like with dark shadows in the deeper areas.

2. Another popular method of colouring plaster is to try to imitate the patina one might find on a bronze. My way of doing this is first to stain the plaster with a black spirit stain. (These stains are obtained from woodworkers' suppliers and are crystals which dissolve in methylated spirit. There are also water-based stains which are equally good but take a long time to dry.) This gets rid of the glaring white of the plaster and because the stain sinks in a small depth, it is more resistant to subsequent scratches. I follow this with several layers of metallic paints, gold, bronze, antique bronze etc. applying each coat patchily so that I get a varied effect. The medium for this will be

cellulose. On top of this, I then apply various coats of oil paint (student quality dissolved in turps), black, Vandyke brown, perhaps a burnt sienna, using a sponge to stipple. Each application must be allowed to dry completely and the work continues until the metallic underlay is totally obliterated. Finally I take a soft cloth lightly dampened with turps and gently pass over the surface until the underlying gold bronze begins to show through in a faint and subtle manner. As soon as I feel pleased with the effect thus obtained, I spray on a light coat of wax polish, thinned with turps, being very careful not to disturb the oil colour. When this is dry, a gentle buffing will give the surface a pleasant glow, and to finish off I frequently dust the whole cast over with French chalk into which I have mixed a little terre verte powder colour. This settles in the crevices and gives the effect of the verdigris that we sometimes observe on bronze casts. If, alternatively, you wished to imitate a terracotta effect, do not use metallic paint but simply brush on layer after layer of oil colours sympathetic to terracotta, such as earth red, raw sienna, yellow ochre, red ochre, etc., possibly stippling, and finishing off with a light spray of wax polish. With any method it is a good idea to have an example of an antique patina in front of you to copy from.

3. I have on occasion treated plaster by coating it with hot linseed oil, until it will take no more, wiping back any stickiness with a cloth dampened with turps, and then giving a light sealing coat of wax polish to finish. This will produce a yellow/brown colour, darkening as the oil is heated over and over again. It also hardens the cast to some degree and renders it virtually waterproof.

Note: in all of the abovementioned treatments, the essential thing is to be sure that the plaster is bone dry to begin with, and take plenty of time over the work. Rome was not built in a day, so where colouring is concerned, never do today what you can put off until tomorrow, otherwise you might end up with a muddy result.

2 · Reproduction Moulding
Making moulds which will give more than one cast

'Piece moulds'

The oldest method of making moulds from which multiple casts could be struck was the so-called 'piece mould' method. This is now outdated, having been replaced by methods using various types of flexible rubber, and I personally have made only one or two such moulds, so I am obliged to limit myself to a mere description of the method in brief. In this type of mould the original model, whether clay, plaster or marble, is divided up, using clay walls, into a large number of pieces, known as 'tesserae' (an old Latin word meaning small block, e.g. mosaic), in such a way that each piece will draw off the surface without locking against its adjacent pieces. Each tessera also has a wire attached to it to provide a grip. Once the whole surface has been covered with these multitude sections, an overall mother mould or jacket has to be added, through which all the grip wires are left protruding. When the mother mould is removed, each tessera is slotted into place, the cast is made and the pieces will come away, one by one, to be used over and over again. If you look carefully at any cast of an antique statue, you will see a multitude of fine raised lines that have been left showing, which are the seams around the aforesaid tesserae.

As will be seen from my brief description, this means of making casts is very complicated and requires great skill and experience. I doubt if it is much in use nowadays. In fact, the best known company in Britain who used this method extensively to make reproductions of important antique statuary, Messrs. Brucciani of London, went out of business around the time of the First World War.

Gelatine Moulds

The best method, in my opinion, for making moulds in the *most economical* way, is to use calves' foot gelatine, sometimes sold as powdered glue size. The method is as follows.

The model or pattern, which is normally plaster, must be well sealed by the application of a dilute coat of shellac, followed by two coats of full strength shellac, giving a glossy surface. On top of this, it is important to apply a coat of thick oil. My preference is for ordinary engine oil. Anything thinner, such as '3 in 1', is not suitable.

This done, lay the model on its side and place a wooden board vertically against its base. Surround the model with a broad bed of clay about 4in. (10cm) wide and thick enough to rise up to the halfway level on the model. It is not necessary to press this hard up against the model at this stage, but its top surface must be smooth. Next prepare some sheets of quite firm clay about ½in. (13mm) thick and lay these lightly all over the model, making sure that you do not place them too far out at baseline. Then make a thin roll of clay, as thick as a finger, and lay it along the baseline and up across the vertical board. This serves to create a press-in edge when the mould, hereafter referred to as the 'shell' or 'case', is complete. After this, place a cone of clay at the highest point of the model in the shell to create an opening or sprue, through which we will pour the gelatine. Finally, place small stumps of clay, pencil thick, standing vertically up from the other 'high points' of the model, to make air escapes through the case.

Having completed this operation, add a layer of plaster about ½in. (13mm) thick, *with scrim*

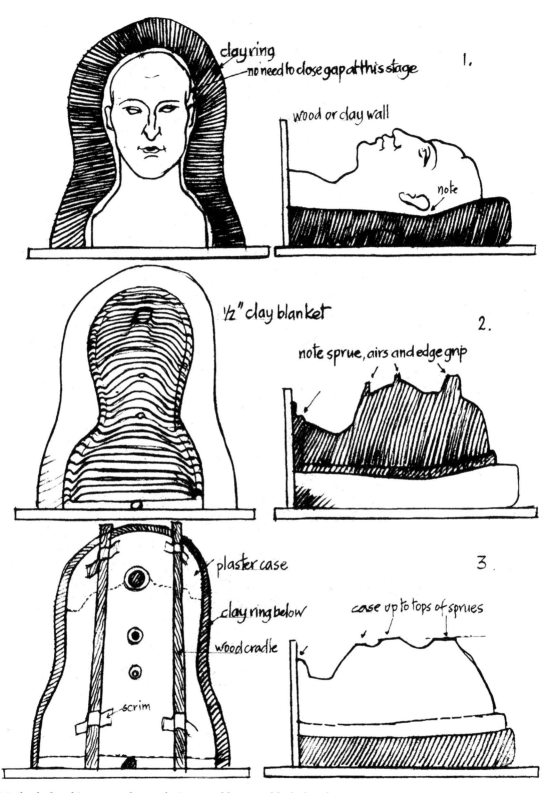

Method of making a case for a gelatine or rubber mould of a head

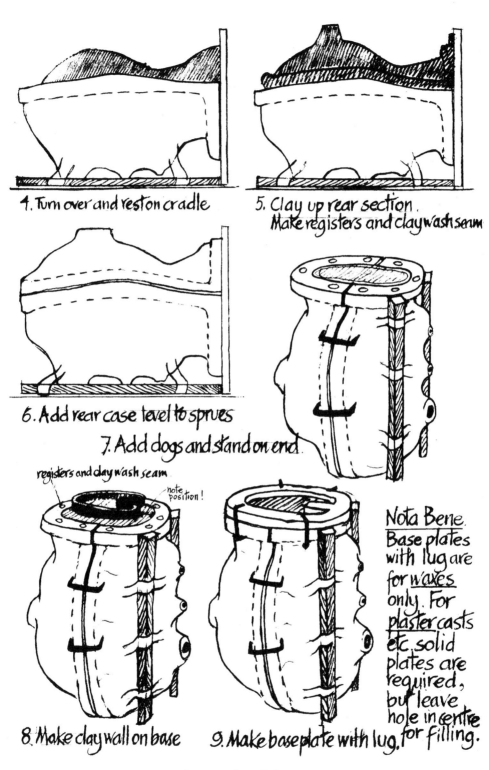

4. Turn over and rest on cradle

5. Clay up rear section.
Make registers and clay wash seam

6. Add rear case level to sprues

7. Add dogs and stand on end.

registers and clay wash seam

note position!

Nota Bene.
Base plates with lug are for _waxes_ only. For plaster casts etc. solid plates are required, but leave hole in centre for filling.

8. Make clay wall on base

9. Make baseplate with lug.

Case completed, ready to open and prepare for gelatine

(and in a large mould perhaps a reinforcing bar) because the mould will be subjected to force later on and must be strong. Smooth the plaster up to the top of the sprue and air vents and be sure that it is wide enough all round to take dog clips later. Then turn the whole thing over, remove the clay bed and cut register holes on the seam. The next move is to repeat the operation as for the first half, i.e. add a clay layer with side grip and sprue and vents, followed by a strong plaster case.

The last job is to remove the wooden baseboard, make registers on the seam, add clay wash, and then make a plaster base plate to take the place of the wooden board. **Note**: it is not necessary to cover the entire base in a large or wide mould. Instead make a clay wall in a ring in the middle and surround it with plaster thus creating a circular base with a space in the centre. Naturally this ring must be wide enough to cross the clay and make contact with the bottom of the model, otherwise the gelatine will escape through the gap. If we are moulding a head that has a flat zone at the base to give the correct angle for setting up later, we will find that our plaster base ring rests against this and thereby gives the correct angle in the subsequent cast. We must check that we have, in fact, not failed to see this point.

This completes the case, and all that remains is for us to add, for a large mould, a simple wooden cradle to one side so that the mould will be stable. Small moulds do not need a cradle and a couple of small lumps of plaster will suffice to stop the tendency to roll about. Now carefully remove one side only of the case, clean it if necessary and coat it on the inside with shellac until it shines. Also oil it with thick oil, but it is better to do this just prior to pouring the gelatine. Then strip away the clay covering the model, close tight the gap around the model and check that the surface is adequately oiled. Then replace the shell, having oiled it, and clamp it down with dogs, not forgetting to clamp also the base plate. Now pour the gelatine through the sprue until it flows from the air vents. (See

below for preparation.) Stop the flow from the vents by pressing a small lump of oiled clay against it. **Note**: that in order to allow for the natural shrinkage in the cooling gelatine, we add an extension to the sprue in the form of a cone-shaped ring of clay, oiled so that it peels off afterwards. This gives that extra inch or two (2.5–5cm) of height. When the gelatine has cooled completely, cut off this extra sprue, turn the mould over and repeat for the other side, removing the half case, shellacking it, removing the clay layer, oiling all surfaces, clamping back the case and pouring the second gelatine.

The final task is simply to open the mould. This must be done with care, removing the base plate first, followed by the two sides of the case. The gelatine should not come away with the case, but should be removed from the model with real care and attention so that there is no risk of its dragging details off the model at the same time. I have on occasion found difficulty in opening the case, generally because I have not oiled it adequately. The only thing you can do if this happens, is to force off one side, then remove the gelatine from that side, replace the case, turn the mould over and press down on the other side by pushing a wooden rod, such as the handle of a hammer, into the sprue. This will exert pressure against the gelatine and force it down into the space below, thus freeing it from its case, but try to avoid such heavy handed work by making a good case in the first place. Once we have freed the gelatines from their case, it is normal practice to clear the oiliness by dusting it with French chalk. (Talcum powder is the same thing.) Whenever we wish to store a gelatine we *must* put it on its model, replace the case and base and fit dog clips as gelatine dries out easily. In any case we cannot expect more than a week or so of life out of a gelatine, whereas rubber moulds are virtually permanent.

Preparing Gelatine for Use

Calves' foot gelatine used to be available in flat cakes, but nowadays it is more likely to be found as powdered glue size. Whichever form we have, it is first necessary to soak it in water overnight so that it turns to a rubbery consistency. As we make our case we then put the gelatine in a double boiler (saucepans will do for this) and heat it to melting. My own way of judging the correct density of the gelatine is to note its colour; light brown would mean a very weak mould, dark brown would be too tough to be flexible; so aim at what I would call a mid-brown.

It is normal practice when the gelatine has been taken out of its case to dry off the oil with French chalk and then brush the surface with alum solution. Since gelatine is a protein, the alum will harden it a little. Whenever I take a wax from a gelatine, I do not bother to use alum and I have not found any problem. It is always more difficult to take a plaster from a gelatine, as the gradual heat emitted by the setting plaster penetrates deeply into the mould surface and makes it go sticky – hence the advisability of alum.

After you have finished with the mould, it is important to cut the gelatine up into small pieces ready for re-melting on a future occasion. The most effective way to do this is to place a sharp knife in a bench vice with the blade facing away from you. You can then draw the gelatine across it easily and safely, thus reducing it to small squares. Storage is important also, as gelatine, being a natural product, is likely to go mouldy if left in a closed or damp place. The best way to keep it is in a paper sack with the top open, and check it every so often. Otherwise it can be laid out on a board until it is completely dried out. These minor inconveniences in the use and the storage of this material have to be balanced against the fact that gelatine is not expensive, and can be melted over and over again in warm water, and provided we avoid mildew it will last a life time.

Rubbers and Vinyls

The more modern materials based on rubbers or vinyls need less attention in the handling and care, and of course will store safely for long periods. The drawbacks are as follows:

- The hot melt rubbers require a special heater that is very expensive to buy and costly in electricity to run. They can be re-melted, but the fact that they shrink, however little, in cooling from their melting point of about 300°C means that they do not fit as tightly in the case as gelatine. As we have already seen, the melting temperature of gelatine is less than 100°C and we should always allow it to cool to touchable heat before pouring it into the case. That way there is virtually no shrinkage.
- The cold, catalysed rubbers do not shrink, of course, and are capable of giving an excellent print, even better than gelatine, since they are poured directly onto the model without there being any shellac or oil to dull the details. However, they are very expensive and cannot be re-used. It is possible, in order to economise, to shred an old rubber mould and mix the result into new rubber to bulk it out for economy, but this will make the mould slightly less flexible.
- All the rubbers have one big advantage – that is they are so tough that they will not be damaged by hot wax or resin or plaster, etc., and in general do not need a release agent, even though I have found it useful to brush a little wax polish onto the mould surface before taking a plaster or a resin cast. Wax casts do not need release.

How does one decide which material to choose? My advice would be to have gelatine always available but to use cold rubbers for those jobs where you are likely to wish to store the mould for future use, or for those occasions where you are casting something with such fine detail, like a coin or medallion, that the necessary coating of shellac/oil for a gelatine mould might obliterate the detail. Before going on to describe the method of moulding with more than two half cases, it might be worthwhile recording a traditional method of storing a gelatine for future use. This method is probably not used by anybody these days but even as an anachronism it is worth mentioning for historical purposes, as it might serve a useful purpose one day and it would be a pity to lose it altogether.

Odd Half Case Moulds

This system was known by the name of 'odd halves', and consisted of plaster casts struck from a gelatine mould in a special way, as follows. Make the case and gelatine and strike off whatever casts are required. Before cutting up the gelatine, lay the two halves of the mould on the bench, apply whatever release agent is needed (almost certainly wax polish), and line each half with plaster, as if we were wishing to make a plaster cast. BUT continue the plaster beyond the edge of the gelatine and over the seams of the case (having added a release agent – perhaps oil or clay wash). When these odd halves, as we may call them, have set, remove them from the mould and replace them against the case, locking each one with dogs. The resultant separate halves may now be stored permanently and the gelatine cut up.

At any future time, if we wish to recreate our gelatine mould all we have to do is to shellac

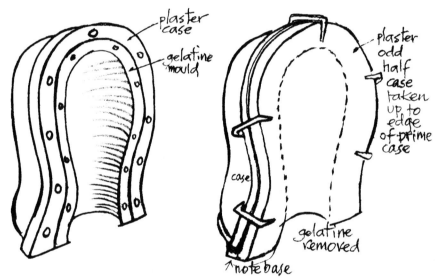

Odd half case moulds

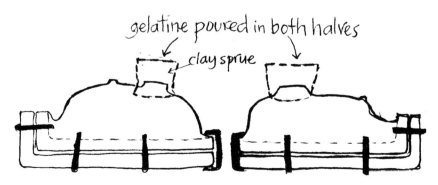

Odd half cases set up ready for recreating moulds of head in gelatine, both poured at the same time

and oil each half case, melt the gelatine and pour each half at the same time, thus recreating the mould we started off with. As mentioned above, this system is now merely a memory and these days, if we wish to store moulds for future use, we make them of rubber, ignoring the cost, or we simply store the original plaster pattern and then make a new case and mould as we require it. (See illustration on page 32.)

Making Cases off Figures

The previous description of making cases for gelatine or rubber casts took a head as an example and was thus a description of a two-part mould. However, to cast a figure or some other form that is more complex than the relative simplicity of a head, then we have to go about the task with a little more forethought and circumspection.

The principal difference however lies in the fact that we are likely to have to make the case in more than two pieces, as even a small figure can require six or seven sections. It is not really possible to give a clear description of the method of making a complex case, but the guiding principle in designing a case is to be sure that each section will draw off the model easily, that is, no part should be so far round the form that pulling off would trap the model inside and break it. This, in fact, simply means that where it looks that a case section is not likely to pull off with ease, then we must make a seam and split the case into smaller pieces. It is not necessary to have the gelatine inside split also into so many pieces, because being flexible it will peel off the model anyway. Therefore a six-part case, for example, might have only two or three parts in its gelatine or rubber. In practice, if you start to make your first section on a wide and simple area of your figure, then all the other pieces will fall into place. Simply make sure the seams of all your sections are upstanding sufficiently off the surface to be able to accept dog clips firmly, otherwise you will have the devil's own job in holding them in the correct position later, and do not forget to cut good register holes or notches in each piece.

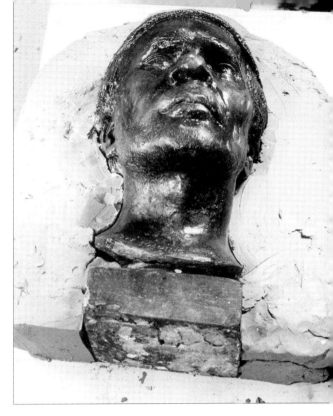

Making a case mould of a head.
Stage 1 'Claying up'. Clay bed to half line

Stage 2 Upper half clayed up. Note sprues

Stage 3   Upper case completed. Note wood rails

Stage 4   Mould reversed and other half being clayed
up ½" (13mm) thick

If you are intending to make the mould of rubber rather than of gelatine, then you will not need a separator. This does save time and also a few pence. However, I would advise a touch of release agent, perhaps wax polish, as the sheer suction of the cold set rubbers especially can often drag quite large bits off the plaster model. I have seen more damage done to models in this way, in foundries who use rubbers, than I have ever experienced with the more gentle gelatine (provided the case and model have been shellacked and oiled, of course).

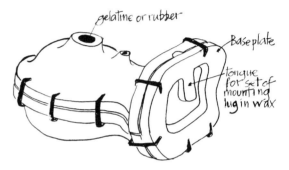

Case mould for head. *Note: base may be flat or angled to base of neck. Also note open base and tongue to give accurate setting of lug on wax and hence on bronze without subsequent weld.*

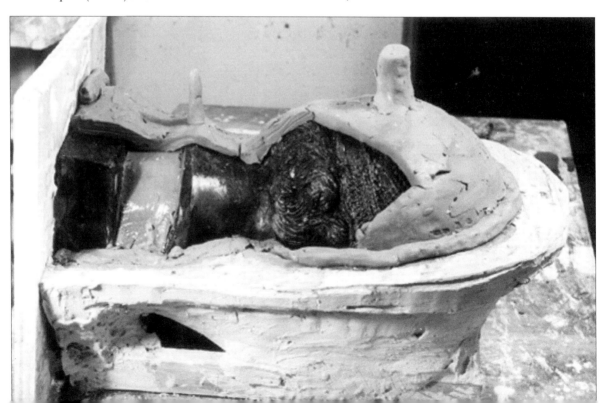

Stage 5   Case made, one half shellacked

Stage 6   Pouring gelatine. Case and model well oiled

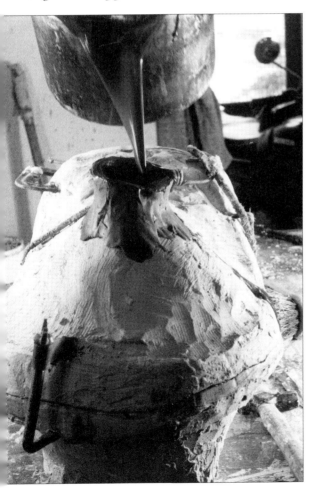

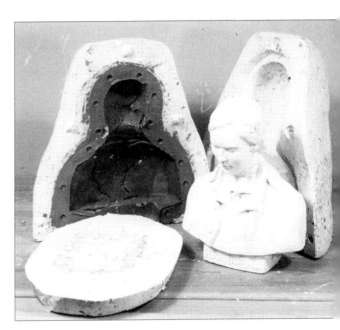

Case mould of a small bust showing rear section
clayed up. Mould to be made in Silastic for multiple
reproductions

Cold Cast Rubbers

These days it is possible to buy cold set rubbers that are painted directly onto the surface of the model; first all over with a viscous but fairly liquid mix and then with a more dough-like material. When a sufficient thickness has been built up, the case is made on top of this, then opened up and the rubber cut with a sharp knife into its separate sections. This seems to be acceptable as a method, but its obvious drawbacks are that it cannot have edge grips to hold the rubber tight against the case. This presents the risk of a seam slipping out of place and therefore giving a poor cast. This should never happen with a case that has been made in the orthodox way, but if a method works well and saves time and effort then I would be the first to include it in my repertoire.

Quite clearly such a method of applying rubber to the surface and making the case afterwards is the best way of making a mould from something such as an antique statue, or a relief attached to a wall, where there is no way that we can lay the model down on the bench to form a case around it. The availability of these modern surface rubbers has put the final nail in the coffin of the old method of piece moulding, and none shall lament its passing.

Another advantage of using the cold cast rubbers is that in certain instances it is possible, using the abovementioned procedure, to make the mould directly off a clay model, thus eliminating the work involved in making a plaster. This in some cases would be worthwhile, in others not. We must choose from all the possibilities open to us, the particular method of working that is most appropriate to the job in hand, and then live with the results.

Left
Pouring cold set Silastic into a small case mould

Below
Wax mould, plaster model and bronze cast of medallion

Two-piece mould in rubber and plaster cast, size 10″ (25.4cm)

Six-piece mould in hot melt rubber, size 10″ (25.4cm)

3 · Modelling Directly in Plaster or Cement

There are occasions when it might be preferable to make a work directly in plaster, in preference to modelling in clay and then casting. I have used this method myself and have seen students use it often enough, although it should be said that it is not necessarily quicker or better to model directly. However, we might at some time wish to adopt this practice and it is worth including it in our discussion. The most important thing to consider when modelling directly is that we must have the maximum freedom to cut into the surface of the work as we progress and therefore we have to avoid anything that will hinder us in this such as scrim bindings, wires or other metals too close to the surface. Moreover, we do not want to have our plaster so hard that our attempts to cut through it merely cause it to break up.

I would therefore suggest that we work in the following way. First, we must make a strong armature of metal, as accurate as possible, but taking care not to make it so big that it comes close to the surface, leaving little or no room for a good covering of plaster. I would suggest that the only way to be sure of doing this properly is to prepare a good maquette beforehand and take careful measurements from that. Some people weld up the armature, but if a welding plant is not available, it is quite in order to bind the metals together with wire, as we do when we wish to make an internal armature in a cast. Next, we might add some chicken netting to create a hollow inside the work, but we must be most careful to keep this extremely small, so that there is no danger of its coming near to the surface at any point.

From here on we work in plaster, not ordinary or standard plaster straight from the bag, but for the first layer, a mixture with about 50% wood shavings. This will make a fibrous mixture, easily poked into the holes in the chicken netting until all the armature is covered, except for the hands and feet or similar thin areas (perhaps including the head) which we leave bare at this early stage. As this soft fibrous mixture hardens we can easily cut into it to begin to block out the large forms of the figure, referring to our maquette as we work.

The next layer will be a mixture with about 50% sawdust stirred into the plaster to a porridge-like consistency and applied by hand, shaping as we proceed. As each layer follows, increase the proportion of plaster, so that the mixture becomes ever more dense and firm, but never so hard that we have to hack violently at it to cut it into shape.

As we approach the final surface, we use only plain plaster, so that the last skin is at the maximum degree of strength. The underlying layers will not, of course, be as strong as pure plaster but as they dry out they will be hard enough, and anyway, the real strength of the work must be in the armature. You will find that this method of working is highly effective and because we have been careful not to put in our mix scrim or other substances which cannot be cut or shaped later, we have given ourselves the maximum facility for modelling an otherwise rather intractable material.

As far as the small details such as hands and feet are concerned, I would not attempt to model them directly in plaster, but would make

Life-sized group, modelled directly in Portland cement by a student at the University of Northern Nigeria, 1962

them in clay, cast them in the normal way and attach them to the armature later. However, at the end of the work you must ask yourself if it would not have been just as quick to make the whole thing in clay and then cast it.

It is possible to apply the abovementioned method to the production of a work in *cement*, rather than plaster and the same procedure would be followed, using pure cement with no sand, mixed, as above, with wood shavings and sawdust. The result will be strong (but less so than cast concrete which contains sand) and has the advantage of being waterproof and therefore exhibitable out of doors. With this method it is important to keep the work *wet* all the time, and to do any cutting back or reshaping before the mixture has set fully. Equally, we cannot expect to put more than a limited amount of cement on at any time, as each layer has to be allowed to set, or part set, before any more is added. Also, as mentioned before, we cannot use sand in the mix or we will find we cannot cut it back. What is more, sand makes the mixture less sticky and thus more likely to keep falling off as we work.

It would seem in the long run that the best way to produce a work in cement is to model it in clay and then cast it. I will describe below how to go about this. My own experience of modelling in cement dates entirely from the years I spent in West Africa, teaching in a University Department of Fine Art, where we did not have any plaster for casting and where the local tradition made much use of cement as a modern replacement for mud. I found it an excellent medium in the circumstances and the students under my care produced some high quality work on a large scale.

Funeral monument in cement, Umuiaha, Nigeria

40

4 · Casting in Cement

A more likely procedure for making works suitable for outdoors, where there are insufficient funds for bronze, would be to make a waste mould in plaster from a clay original and cast from it, either in cement or in resin. I do not much like either of these materials, but they are cheap, relatively easy to use and at one time were very popular. I think it goes without saying that they only make sense for large works. Small pieces are probably better in terracotta.

The method of casting in cement is almost identical to that for plaster casting, except that we have to remember that cement has to be packed into the mould, bit by bit. Therefore we must design the sections so that we have easy access to all corners as we cannot rely on pouring the mixture into deep places. The other way in which a waste mould for cement might differ is that it should be a little thicker than a similar mould for plaster, simply because we

Funeral monument in cement, Ikot Ekpene, Nigeria

will get better results if we hammer the cement against the mould to knock out air pockets and this does subject it to great strain. As a separator, I would recommend shellac and wax, applied generously to a part-dried mould. Remember to dampen it again afterwards and keep it well dampened until the work is finished.

The first layer of cement should be applied as a thick cream, brushed onto the surface. This should not contain any sand. Do not wait for this to set, but proceed with the next application, this time containing about 50% sand, pressed gently against the first layer in small quantities at a time. Then, as the mixture starts to harden, tamp it down with a hammer or similar tool. This will probably be followed by a third layer, but it is not necessary to make a very thick cast. I have often made cement casts no more than ½in. (13mm), but of course you must insert plenty of reinforcing irons.

One difficulty you may experience in cement casting is that there is an annoying tendency for the mixture to slide away from the vertical parts of the mould and pile up at the bottom in the hollows. If this happens, it means that your mixture is too wet, but it is possible to overcome this by adding an accelerator, such as Febspeed, which will cause the cement to set fast, even in minutes. I find this is useful for packing the seams later when the upper parts of the mould have been put in place and you have to press the cement into downward facing seams. Equally it is invaluable for the work of filling up open seams or other defects on the surface afterwards, where instant setting is essential.

Once your mould is filled, keep it wet for a day or so, then chip out as for plaster, patch any bad areas, let it dry out completely and finally give it a good waxing. Normally we would use fondu ciment for castings, as it has a better colour than grey Portland, and sets faster. However, we can add powder colour to ordinary cement if we wish. In either case we should not forget to reinforce the cast with strong iron bars, well-treated with anti-rust paint, especially if we wish to place our cast outdoors. I recall on one occasion adding a quantity of bronze powder to my gel coat in a fondu ciment cast, which, as time went by, gave a pleasing metallic touch to the surface, somewhat in the same way that we aim at when doing a bronze-filled resin cast. However, I am of the opinion that both resin and cement casts are essentially amateur in nature, and while an art student might use them as an expedient, for example for a large work to go outdoors, where funds are limited, such materials are best avoided for small works and all effort should be made to produce bronze casts.

5 · Casting in Glass Fibre Reinforced Resin

The use of glass fibre reinforced resin, either polyester or epoxy, was very popular from the 1960s onwards, and was frequently made to imitate bronze by the addition of bronze powder as a filler in the gel coat, which could later be patinated. In fact, the expression 'cold cast bronze' was often used both by sculptors and by dealers to describe such materials. This was eventually discredited as it gave the impression that these were somehow real bronze casts, made, in some magical way, without heating the metal. Perhaps the best description would be 'resin bronze', since what we are dealing with is nothing more nor less than plastic, and should be seen as such. However, the fact remains that this material is still widely used and it is therefore worthwhile describing the technique of casting with it.

Assuming we have made our original in clay and have made a waste mould from it in the normal way, we should first allow all sections of the mould to dry out sufficiently to be able to take up to three good coats of shellac (note that cellulose or other types of sealant will not work with resin), followed by a coat of good quality wax polish, buffed up to as high a shine as possible. This task must be done with great care, as any poorly sealed areas will allow the resin to pass into the plaster mould and separation will be impossible. Many sculptors make their resin casts from a completely dry mould, arguing that dampness inhibits the setting of the resin, but I have found that a dry mould exerts such enormous osmotic pressure that the shellac barrier does not always work well, and I have therefore always dampened my moulds after

shellacking, with no ill effects. Now we are ready to begin casting.

Prepare the resin mixed with the filler of choice in small quantities (I always found that about a half full jam jar was enough at one time). We might use bronze powder, or preferably a 50/50 mix of bronze and brass, or we may prefer a dry filler such as cement, which gives a grey/black colour, or slate powder for a deep black, or indeed any other material provided we know it will not react chemically with the resin. The manufacturers of resin give instructions as to how much filler ought to be used. However, I have found that their maximum recommendations are on the low side and the finished cast thereby has a tell-tale waxen look about it, so I ignore the instructions and put as much filler as the liquid will take without going too stiff to flow.

Now add your catalyst and stir thoroughly, following the manufacturer's recommendations as to the quantities required. It is normal to work in a warm environment, but as might well be the case, if you have only an unheated studio, you will find that a little extra catalyst added to the mix will help to overcome the otherwise prolonged setting time. Your catalysed mix should now be brushed all over the first section of the mould and allowed time to harden. This is followed by a second coat and all high points should be topped up carefully.

We may now move on to the laborious task of laying up the glass fibre. This is not difficult, but it must be one of life's least enjoyable jobs, as you will soon discover if you try it out. The method is to brush a generous coat of clear resin onto the gel coat and then begin to press the glass into it, with an old paint brush, dabbing vertically until the glass is completely soaked out. Cover the entire section in this manner, building up to at least two, if not three layers, allowing the resin to set after each, and making sure to adequately build up seams. The whole process should then be repeated for each section of the mould in turn. All spillage on seams must be carefully trimmed off. Then begin to reassemble the sections, pouring a little of the gel mix along each seam to seal it and covering it over with patches of glass if we are able to reach into the mould. No reinforcing irons are needed, but I personally put them in anyway, in a large work.

As soon as we have completed the last section we may start the work of chipping out. This at least will be easy as the resin is so hard that it is very resistant to the chisel, and since it does shrink a little in hardening, it comes away from the mould quite readily. Finally we patch any defects on the surface with our gel mix. Then, especially where we have used a metal filler, we rub the whole surface over with fine steel wool. The last job is to wax and buff up, or patinate as for bronze, with reagents. Since the surface of a resin cast contains only a percentage of metal, it will not patinate with the same readiness as true bronze, but nonetheless good colours can be achieved with patience. It is important to ensure that we have rubbed down well with steel wool to expose the bronze powder first of all, and I have found it necessary to apply the reagent a bit stronger than I would do for real bronze. I will give additional recipes in the chapter on bronze casting, but for now I would recommend using a wash of potassium polysulphide as a starter, giving a black/brown colour, perhaps followed by copper carbonate to add a green shade, or if we wish, ferric nitrate for a russet overlay. Finally all that is needed is a good coat of wax polish and a gentle buffing up to a pleasing lustre.

At this point it might be useful to look again at our separators or release agents, as they differ according to the job in hand.

1. Plaster cast from plaster mould	Soap, soda
2. Cement cast from plaster mould	Shellac and wax
3. Resin cast from plaster mould	Shellac and wax
4. Wax cast from plaster mould	No separator but wet mould
5. Plaster cast from gelatine mould	Light wax
6. Wax cast from gelatine mould	Light oil
7. Any material from rubber mould	Light wax.

6 · Bronze Casting by the Lost Wax Process

Perhaps the most common way of producing casts in bronze is for the sculptor to make the original image in plaster and hand it to a commercial foundry that will do the whole casting right up to patination and even mounting on a good display base. This naturally is costly unless we are able to do some of the work ourselves. I have previously described methods of making gelatine or rubber case moulds from which we can take waxes, ready for the foundry, thereby saving some of the expense, and I will now describe other ways of reducing the amount of work to be done by the foundry.

Making a Single Wax Direct from a Waste Mould

Assuming the original to be in clay, first make a plaster waste mould in the usual way, differing only in that here you do not need to use a coloured first layer. Having opened and cleaned the mould, now prepare a pan of melted wax. For this method I would use standard modelling wax (micro-crystalline). Melt it on a low flame and take it up to very hot. The mould must be *wet* otherwise you will find that the hot wax sticks to it. Using a smallish brush, now paint the surface of each mould section, working in a regular and careful way across the surface, not brushing but almost spooning the wax on, and allowing it to spill freely over the seams so that it has a good grip. When all the surfaces are

Examples of plaster waste moulds and 'one off' waxes struck from them (sizes approximately 12" (30cm))

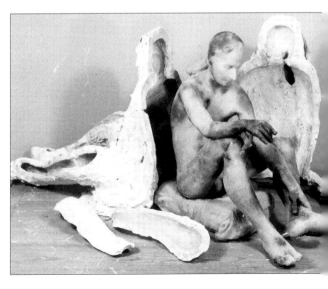

The case – almost complete

Preparation of a case mould on a portrait head

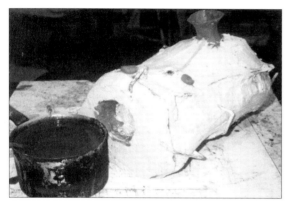

The case ready for gelatine

The wax painted into the mould

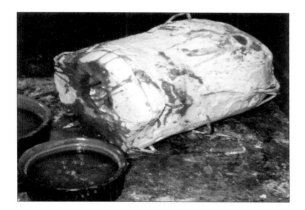

The third coat of wax poured into the mould

The wax cast – shown with the plaster original and the gelatine mould

Making a wax from a gelatine mould

completely covered, begin again, this time with slightly cooler wax, brushing it on gently so that you can clearly see the difference. By now you should have built up about ⅛in. (4mm) thickness.

The next task is to strengthen the high points, that is all areas of the mould that rise up to points or ridges. To do this, prepare some wax in the following way. Having oiled your fingers with olive or other vegetable oil, pour a small amount of the liquid wax onto the surface of a bowl of cold water, wait a few seconds, then gently lift it out and begin squeezing and kneading it vigorously until it acquires the consistency of soft clay and all traces of oil or water have disappeared. Then pinch off a small amount and roll it, pencil thin, on to a board or other flat surface. The resulting rod should then be laid along the high spots of the mould and carefully smoothed down. This means that when the final coat of wax is applied it will not wash off the underlying layer, resulting in thin places in the cast. The same rod of wax should also be attached all around the base or bottom edge of the cast.

Now take a sharp knife and trim away all the wax that has previously been allowed to spill onto the seams and begin to re-assemble the mould, piece by piece, pouring a drop of hot wax into each seam as you go, to seal up from the inside. When the mould is all in place, smear a little clay, or soft wax, along the seams outside to prevent any leakage and knock in a few dogs or, perhaps better, bind the mould with a wire to hold it all together.

Meanwhile, melt a larger pan of wax and let it stand until a skin has just started to form on the surface. There must be sufficient wax in the pan to fill the mould completely, to its top edge. Hold it steady for a few seconds then pour it out again, rolling the mould around as you do so to ensure that as even a layer of wax as possible is deposited. You should now have built about ³⁄₁₆in. (5mm) thickness – less would not allow the metal to flow well and more would result in a very heavy cast.

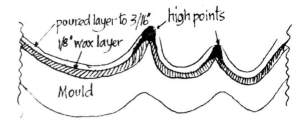

How a wax should be thickened up at its high points, prior to pouring in the final layer (up to ³⁄₁₆″ thick)

Allow a short time for cooling, and then begin to chip out with great care. It is best to do this while the wax is still slightly warm so that it will be a little flexible. The shrinkage in the cast will have released the wax somewhat and chipping out should be relatively easy, but be cautious and resist any temptation to lever off large pieces as so doing might tear the wax inside. When all the mould has been removed, the cast is ready for any further finishing work before proceeding to the foundry.

Waxes up to about 36in. (90cm) high can easily be made in this way, and will be safe in storage, for lengthy periods, provided they are kept well away from a heat source. Works larger than this might prove to be too heavy and could begin to sink under their own weight, so perhaps this method is best reserved for smaller work. In any case, when I make a wax by this means I usually shore up the base walls or similar places, on the inside, with short wax rods as one might buttress a wall, in order to strengthen the cast, both in the chipping out stage and in the later storage. Equally, in the case of a heavy wax on a wide base, or a standing figure, take the precaution of placing a lump of clay inside the base to avoid any danger of the figure collapsing. Another useful thing to do with a standing figure is to provide a couple of external buttresses, from the back of the knee down to the edge of the base, to stop any tendency for the figure to lean out of true.

The (hollow) wax with its gates and cup, ready for investing for bronze

The wax part invested

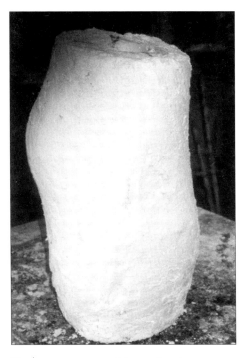

The investment mould completed

The cast removed from the mould

Casting a bronze – four final stages

Striking a Wax from a Gelatine

The method of making a hollow wax from a gelatine or rubber mould differs only in that it is common practice to add a quantity of about 30% to 40% rosin to our final coat of wax, the idea being that such a mixture has a lower freezing point than the micro-crystalline I recommended above, and therefore as it is poured into the mould, it is less likely to melt off any of the underlying wax. Also, as the rosin mix is harder, it does give a slightly stronger result. Many foundries use only hard wax right from the surface, so as to avoid any damage from warm hands later. Hard wax, however, is less suitable when we are working from a waste mould as it often shatters as we are chipping out, whereas micro-crystalline is more flexible.

Wax cast already cored and gelatine mould in its case

The author at work on a wax portrait

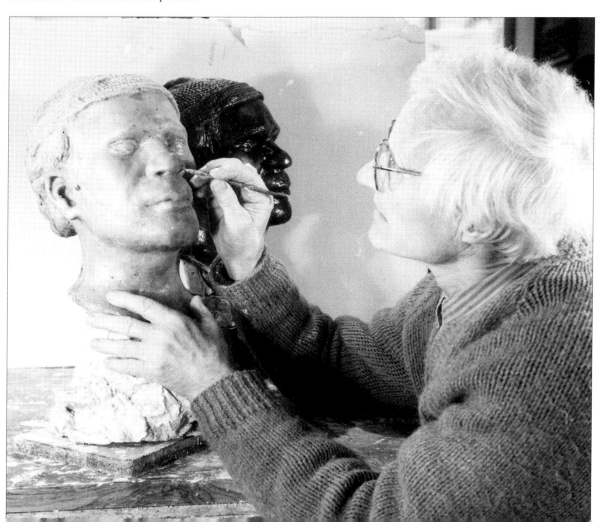

Original model and wax cast supported on its core

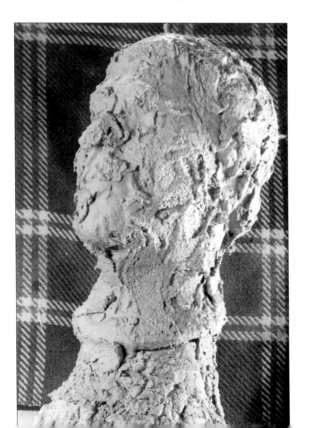

Finished mould ready for firing

Left: Coating the wax with ludo. Note core nails.

Making a Single Wax on a Small Scale

It is more convenient, when we are working on a small scale, perhaps no more than about 8in. (20cm), to model directly in wax, rather than casting from a mould, assuming of course, that we do not want to make an edition. There are two well-known methods of doing this, both of which date back to the most ancient times. One of these is to mould a lump of wax by hand as we would do a lump of clay, and the other is to make a simple 'core' of refractory material onto which we apply our wax. The first method will give us a solid cast, therefore it must be small; the other will be crudely hollow and may therefore be a bit larger but it too has its maximum size.

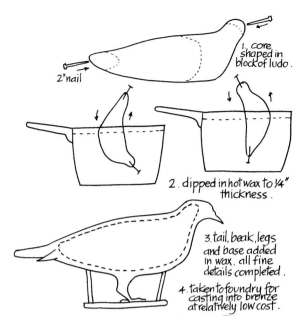

Making a small work in wax on a pre-formed ludo core

A. The first method is as follows. Prepare a pan of modelling wax, heating it up to just melting temperature. Then oil your hands and either pour a small amount of wax on to cold water and mash it to malleable condition, or, as some sculptors prefer, allow it to cool to a paste and then scoop some out of the pan, again mashing it to a workable state. Then shape this lump to as approximate a form as will correspond to the image you intend to make, and allow it to harden completely, Thus you have made a recognizable start. On this simply add more wax, or cut off, either cold or by using a hot spatula, and continue to work until you have achieved the finished image. The limitation to this way of working is determined by the thickness at its greatest point, which should not be allowed to exceed about 1in. (2.5cm). The reason for this is that bronze, in greater mass, will shrink so much on cooling that all surface detail will be lost on one side. This shrinkage is known as *risucchio* or, literally, re-suction and cannot be eliminated. In addition to this, we should note that the thicker the bronze, the heavier will the cast be and naturally will cost more, even though small amounts such as we are speaking about here would not be the end of the world for us.

B. The second method, still much in use in those parts of the world where cottage industry bronze casting goes on, such as India, Africa, the Far East etc., is to make a core to start off, which will give a rough image and also ensure a hollow cast. It is quite possible to use this method even on a large scale, as was the case throughout most of history, before the use of negative moulds came to be common. However, here we are discussing small-scale work, and in any case I personally have no experience in working on a large core as I always cast from a mould. (I have to point out here that this method cannot be used if we are intending to make the cast by the modern ceramic shell process, since it depends on a plaster bound core that is not appropriate in such up-to-date casting.)

The procedure is as follows. The first step is to make up a core mixture. This will be about 50% plaster and the same of fine ground 'grog', or ceramic powder, mixed in water, to a porridge-like consistency. This material is commonly known as 'ludo', or 'investment'. It is virtually the same as the mixture used for making a mould for a bronze in the traditional method, as will be described later. As this mixture starts to stiffen, try to mould it by hand into an approximation of the final image. This will only be approximate, because, as you will soon discover, ludo has no plasticity worth speaking about and can only be drawn into the simplest of shapes, in the short time we have before the plaster binder sets. We cannot add any more ludo later, although we can of course, cut it back with a suitable tool.

Now make up a pan of hot wax, large enough to be able to allow the image to be dipped into it. Next knock a long nail, or, better, a long screw, into one end of the 'core', and using this as a grip, lower the whole thing into the liquid wax, cooling it each time, and repeating until you have coated the core with about ³/₁₆in. (5mm) thickness. If the wax is not too hot, it will be enough to dip about three times, but you can only be really sure of the thickness, by cutting a small piece out of the surface and estimating it by eye. Where there is a flat base to the image, all you have to do is to cut away the wax that has overlapped it and you will see the thickness at once.

The image is now ready to add whatever additional details are desired, using soft wax as before. As I mentioned above, this pre-formed core method is best suited to simple shapes, or equally to images whose additional details do not need to be so massive as to cause us problems of shrinkage. In antiquity, a similar method of working was common, up to any dimension, but clearly a more plastic material was used for the core, so that it could be built up in layers, and the wax could be applied, either by brushing on to the surface, or by laying pre-formed sheets of wax on to it and detailing afterwards. My aim, however, is to discuss small-scale working methods that can be easily done in a modest workshop or studio, as is the practice in the Third World.

As stated before, the aim of this book is to provide information on casting methods which we can easily use in our own workshops or studios with the simplest of tools and equipment, employing traditional materials where they are less costly than those that a

modern commercial foundry might use. It is unlikely, perhaps, that we will have the space to build our own kiln and furnace so that we are able to do our own bronze casts although, for those who do have such space, the equipment for casting on a modest scale can be easily organized, and need not cost you an arm and a leg. I myself have never built anything more advanced than a simple kiln capable of temperatures up to 600°C because I had, in my teaching years, access to my college foundry. It was for many years my sole responsibility and I did all the casting, in all the available materials, for our students, as well as doing my own bronze casting. I will however, later on, describe the method of constructing a burn-out kiln for those who might have space available. For the moment, however, I will describe the methods of preparing waxes and moulds ready for casting.

Castings in non-ferrous metals such as bronze, brass, lead or aluminium, by the lost wax process, can be done by the traditional investment or ludo moulding method, or by the more modern ceramic shell technique.

'Pigeon' modelled and cast by V. Butler 1980

Investment or Ludo Moulding Method

In either case the preparation of the wax model is virtually identical, the differences lying only in the moulding material used and its particular handling. In order to set up a wax for moulding we proceed, therefore, as follows. The first step is to make a quantity of wax rods, by rolling a wax/rosin mix, as described on page 47, on a flat surface, so that we have some finger thick rods and some about half that size or approximately pencil thick. These are to provide entry channels or 'gates' for the metal to enter the mould, and vents (the thinner ones), for the air to exit. We may, if we wish, roll these out of modelling wax. However, the best way is to make a mixture of about 40–50% micro-crystalline and the rest of rosin, as this will give us better rolling qualities, being more plastic and not so 'short' as straight modelling wax often is, and more usefully, it is a lot easier to weld it into our model without dripping or collapsing under its own weight. These rods should be cooled to maximum hardness by keeping them in a bowl of cold water and then attached to the wax in appropriate places to provide inlets for the metal and exits for the air.

It is not possible to describe in words alone the many variations likely in setting up such systems, but a few illustrations will give a general idea, and then trial and error will be the guiding principle, when we set about it for ourselves. Suffice it to say, however, that in general, small works will be cast upside down, so that the gates will largely be attached below the base, together with the vents, in order to have fewer attachments on the surface of the cast; whereas larger works will be cast in an upright position. This general rule varies so much in practice that each cast has to be considered and planned irrespective of fixed rules. It does help, though, to remember that it is gravity that forces the hot metal into the mould and thus we place our gates in the most obvious places to facilitate this, and as the air rises we of course ensure that we place our vents at the uppermost points. In any case, these rods are attached to the surface by welding them on with a hot knife, and doing it quickly so that heat does not start to travel too far in the surrounding area, or else the rods will simply fall off again. In addition to the gating system, we will need to make a sprue, or cup, of wax, to be joined to the top of the gates as a pouring place for the metal. Instead of making these of wax, it is perfectly possible to use discarded plastic or polystyrene cups.

Note: before we attach our gating system, we should place *core pins* in the appropriate positions in the wax. These are short copper, brass or steel pins pushed halfway through the hollow wax which support the core after the mould has been fired and the wax burned off. Each part of the figure should have at least two pins. On large works cut nails can be used instead. Being tapered, these can be pulled out of the metal later with ease. The illustrations below will give an idea of how gating systems might be set up. Note the *direction* of the entry points in their relation to the flow of the metal.

Once you have fixed your gating system and pins in place you would normally cover the upper part with enough ludo to form a block, then reverse the figure in order to complete the gating system up to the pouring cup. However, before you add the cup, you must remember to pour the core in. This is made up of about half and half fine grog and plaster, mixed with water, to a creamy but liquid consistency, and then poured into the opening of one of the legs until it rises up to the other, some being allowed to spill over onto the base to form a grip with the rest of the mould. (To make sure the core rises up to points such as, in our example above, the wrists, a good plan is to have a pin inserted through the wax at the high point, then as you pour in the core you withdraw this and you will see the mixture appearing at the hole as the trapped air escapes.) You should now add the cup and check that the air vents have been brought up level with it (perhaps bridging each one across to the cup edge with a short wax rod so as not to lose sight of them when you make the mould). We may now proceed to make the investment mould as shown by the dotted line in the illustration below.

Before this however we should give a little thought to *core vents*. These are in essence small holes drilled through the wax at various places and penetrating a short distance into the core. The idea is that, as the core is surrounded by the hot metal, it will heat up greatly and air or traces of wax gas left inside it will expand rapidly and blast ragged holes in the cooling metal. Core vents, in theory at least, will channel away this explosive pressure and dissipate it into the porosity of the main mould. Some foundries make quite elaborate core vents using tiny copper tubes to extend the holes into the mould, but I find it is sufficient to do as described above.

Where to place these vents? Difficult to say because we never can be sure where core gases are going to occur, but my practice has always been to site them at those places where I will later be able to make use of them to poke a wire through to knock out the core, subsequently tapping and plugging the hole with bronze. Most of the core will come out through the base, but in the case of figures without an open base, such as a standing figure, an animal etc., we have only the tiny spaces at the ankles to work through, so our core vent holes come into use here and in all places otherwise unreachable through the base. Typical places would be the top of a head, the top of each shoulder, the knee where a leg is bent and so on. It is not harmful to leave cores inside a cast, and many foundries

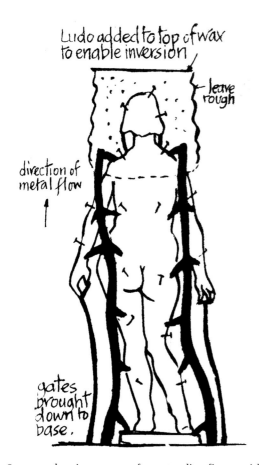

Suggested gating systems for a standing figure with core

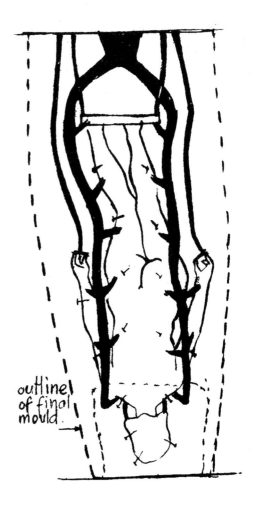

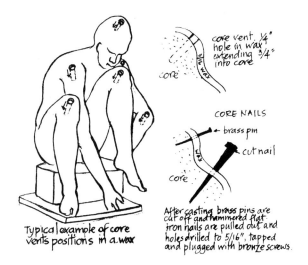

core vent. ¼"
hole in wax
extending ¾"
into core

core

CORE NAILS

brass pin

cut nail

core

After casting brass pins are
cut off and hammered flat.
iron nails are pulled out and
holes drilled to 5/16", tapped
and plugged with bronze screws.

Typical example of core
vents positions in a wax

do just that, but somehow it seems bad craftsmanship not to clear out as much as one can.

Where we are making very small works, solid cast without cores, we do not usually have core nails or vents. Also, the gating system will be simpler as we do not need to feed the metal flow over core surfaces, but simply pour it into an open mould, so that it is usually enough to attach one or two heavy gates directly onto the base of the wax. Normally we would increase the thickness of the gates as this helps to overcome the shrinkage in the cast. Some foundries occasionally insert a short length of bronze rod into the thickest part of a solid wax, very much like a core nail, the idea being that this causes rapid cooling in the metal and so overcomes the problem of *risucchio*, but whether it really works or not is hard to say with certainty, but then every cook has his particular whim, so if you find it works for you then go on doing it. You will have to drill out the 'cooler' in any case as it will not fuse with the bronze, and plug it in the same way as we plug vent holes.

Making the Mould

The mould, whether for bronze, lead or aluminium, will be made of investment; a mixture, for the first facing layer, of about 50% fine ground grog with plaster. The second layer will be of rougher ground grog – birdseed size is

very good for this (although some foundries use ¼ in. (6mm) to dust) – and the final outer layers will be of previously used mould material crushed to powder and bound with about 30% plaster, commonly referred to as 'ludo'.

The facing layer should be applied, fairly liquid, with a soft brush, after first spraying the wax all over with methylated spirit, which acts as an attractive for the coating and helps to ensure a thorough penetration to all details. This facing coat is taken more or less up to the tops of the core nails, that is about ¾ in. (19mm) in thickness, and left rough so as to key with the following layers. After this make up a mixture of medium grog with about 30–40% plaster, not too liquid, and build it up to completely cover all the gates and the cup. Finally, prepare a quantity of ludo and complete the mould to *at least* 1in. (2.5cm) more all round.

The top of the mould should be scraped flat and we must be sure that we can see all the air vents. For a big mould it is good practice to surround it with a cage of chicken netting, well-bedded into the final layer of ludo, because investment moulds are extremely fragile when fired and have been known to break in pieces on handling.

We are now ready to fire out the mould in a kiln. It will be placed, cup downwards, on the kiln bed and the burners set to a medium flame, with the aim of raising the temperature to about 600°C overnight. These six to eight hours will have removed all steam from the mould and the bulk of the wax also. Continue firing, keeping the temperature about the same and after maybe another two hours or so we begin to see strong flames issuing from the mouth of the mould. Our kiln must always be so arranged as to allow us to look inside at base level. Continue to fire until all sign of flame has died away. This can take a surprising amount of time, but it is most important that *all* the gases in the mould have been burnt away, otherwise we will undoubtedly have a disastrous cast.

Now cool the mould until it can be handled, which will take many hours, according to the size of the mould. Then transport it, with great care, to the pouring area, blow away any dust from the cup area with bellows or a rubber tube, settle it in the pit and prepare the metal.

Fire the metal up to its recommended melting temperature – bronze just short of 1200°C, brass about 1150°C, aluminium 700°C and lead about 300°C. The metal suppliers will give precise temperatures to guide you. I personally prefer to work without a pyrometer and make my judgement by eye. With bronze and brass we need to add a good handful of charcoal to the crucible when we have reached melting point. This is stirred in vigorously and then, if we wish, we add a de-gassing agent, although some foundries use only charcoal. Having removed the crucible from the furnace, now skim off the dross, allow the heat to reduce a little, to around 1150°C for bronze and 1100°C for brass, and then pour. The freezing time for bronze is short and as soon as the cup has darkened we may dig out the mould from the pit, and leave it in the atmosphere to go completely cold, prior to opening it up. Lead, surprisingly, takes quite a time to cool, so we need to be quite sure it is safe to open up. The cast is then taken on to the workbench and the gates sawn off close, ready for the final finishing processes. The mould material can be stored in a dry place for future re-use.

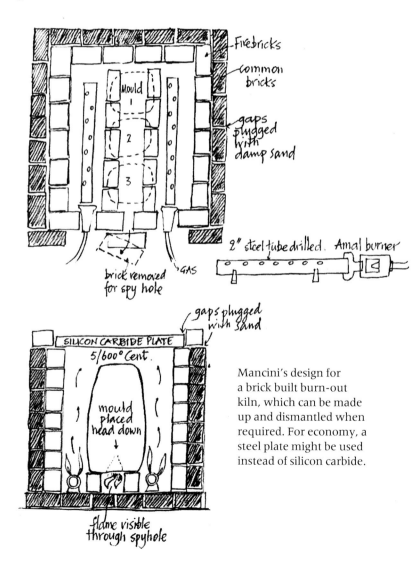

Mancini's design for a brick built burn-out kiln, which can be made up and dismantled when required. For economy, a steel plate might be used instead of silicon carbide.

Laing's Foundry, Edinburgh

Pouring the bronze into the mould (1050°C).
Laing's Foundry, Edinburgh

Alistair Laing in the foundry, 1993

57

A small work in wax showing a typical gating system (height 10" (25.4cm))

Where we have an open base, we will be able to remove most of the core through it; enclosed cores and all small details will have to be cleaned out through the vent holes in the way described earlier. All mould residue on the surface of the cast will come off with wire brushes. At one time it was common to steep casts in weak hydrochloric acid to loosen the mould residue and any slag stuck to the bronze, but I personally found that it was very difficult to get rid of the acid afterwards, which can leave whitish, salt deposits on the patinated surface.

The examples we have looked at so far have suggested that the core should be poured into the hollow wax *after* removing it from its mould, mostly after having attached the gate system and core pins. There are some occasions, however, when it is more convenient to insert the core *before* the mould (whether gelatine or waste mould) is opened up. A typical example of such a procedure would be in the case of a head, as follows. Having painted the wax and closed up the mould, we attach gates from the base edge, all round, together with the air vents, attach a cup and then pour in the core. Since a head is clearly a large open space inside with no narrow spaces to fill, we must make our core mixture of ludo, that is 30% plaster and 70% crushed investment, avoiding the addition of rough grog which could give us a hard and unyielding core that will not crush down as the bronze cools around it, and perhaps lead to cracks in the cast. The core can be built up around the gates and cup, levelled off to form a flat top and allowed to set. Then the whole thing is turned over, the case and gelatine removed, or the waste mould chipped off, and we have the wax, already cored and gated, requiring only finishing work, if we wish it, before we knock in the core pins and then complete the mould for firing.

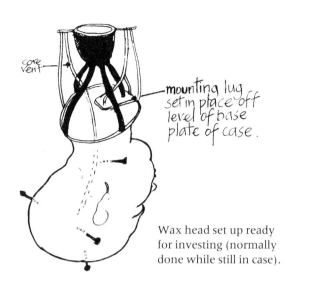

core vent

mounting lug set in place off level of base plate of case.

Wax head set up ready for investing (normally done while still in case).

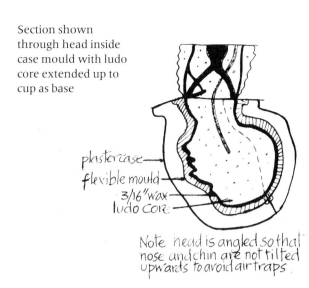

Section shown through head inside case mould with ludo core extended up to cup as base

plaster case
flexible mould
3/16" wax
ludo core

Note head is angled so that nose and chin are not tilted upwards to avoid air traps

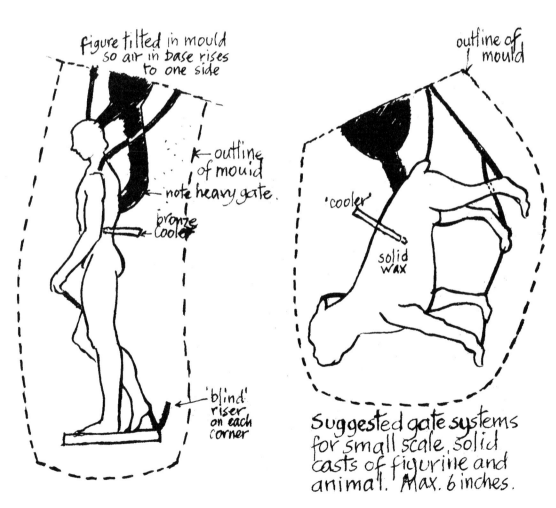

figure tilted in mould so air in base rises to one side

outline of mould

note heavy gate.

bronze cooler

'blind' riser on each corner

outline of mould

'cooler'

solid wax

Suggested gate systems for small scale, solid casts of figurine and animal. Max. 6 inches.

Suggested gate systems for small-scale solid casts of figurine and animal (maximum height 6″ (15cm))

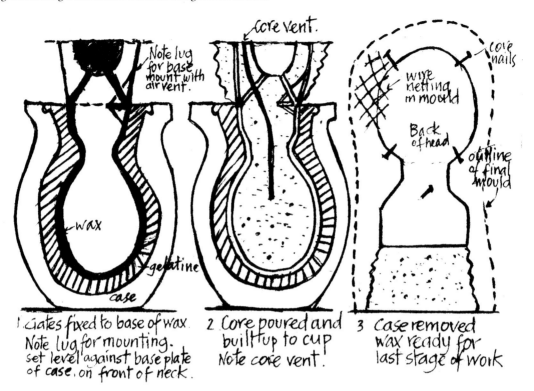

1 Gates fixed to base of wax. Note lug for mounting. set level against base plate of case, on front of neck.

2 Core poured and built up to cup. Note core vent.

3 Case removed wax ready for last stage of work

Core Vents

I previously spoke of core vents, describing them as simple holes drilled through the wax and extending into the core. I have always found that these work quite satisfactorily, but there are alternatives which I have used often enough myself. Some foundries use a short length of stainless steel tube pushed through the wax. This also serves as an extra core nail, and being of tough metal can be drawn out easily after casting and utilised over and over again. Another method is to use a copper tube, although it will not easily survive more than one or two times, but being soft, it can be drilled along its length in the manner of a flute, so as to increase its efficiency – at least in theory. It must be filled up with wax, of course, before being inserted into the core otherwise it will choke up with ludo and not work. Finally, there are core vents that are inserted through the open end of a wax, either as the core is setting or by drilling a hole downwards. A common method of making such a core vent is to soak a length of string in wax, then spiral it round a piece of wire which stiffens it for pushing into half set core mixture. In some cases it is just as easy to insert a length of wax without wire, provided we do not break it in so doing. In all cases the top end of the vent is taken up with a wax rod to the top of the mould and must not touch other vents or the bottom of the cup.

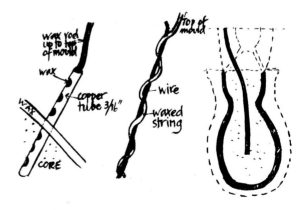

Typical core vents

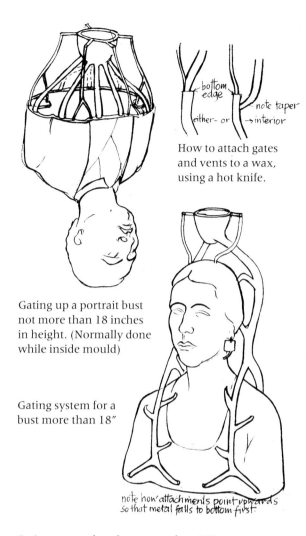

How to attach gates and vents to a wax, using a hot knife.

Gating up a portrait bust not more than 18 inches in height. (Normally done while inside mould)

Gating system for a bust more than 18″

note how attachments point upwards so that metal falls to bottom first.

Gating system for a bust more than 18″

Chasing a Bronze

After having dealt with the core, and having cut off all gates and plugged the core holes, we may now turn our attention to the task of reducing the stumps to a level surface. This is done with a sharp chisel, followed by hammering down flat, then discreet matting with a matting tool to remove shininess. It may be that we also have 'flashing' or 'feathering' on the surface, where cracks in the mould have filled with a sharp crest of metal. This is chased in the same way and matted down to invisibility. Any signs of porosity in the cast will be gently hammered away and matted likewise, and if we wish, we can redefine parts of the detail by chiselling and filing, until we feel satisfied. Chasing can be a lengthy, but very enjoyable business and it is a pleasant experience to see how the bronze begins to come to life as we work at it.

Patinating a Bronze

Adding a patina to a bronze is simply a matter of washing the surface with chemicals, which will combine with the copper to give rich and varied colours. This again is a lengthy and tedious task, as different layers need to be added and then given time to work, perhaps washing off in between each. When we feel satisfied with our achieved colour, we finish by warming the cast on a gas flame to sweat out moisture and then brushing very lightly with a good quality wax polish.

Patination Methods

There are dozens of recipes available for patinating a bronze, and each foundry has its own favourites. However, it will be useful to look at a few basic preparations, which may be developed and changed with experience.

Basic black/brown	Potassium polysulphide solution
Basic green	Copper chloride
Basic grey/green	Mercuric chloride
Basic russet	Ferric nitrate
Basic blue/green	Copper sulphate with acetic acid

It is very important that the bronze be completely clean and grease-free before brushing on the reagent. Some of the abovementioned chemicals will work cold (mercuric chloride and potassium polysulphide in particular), but all work more effectively with heat. However, note that the degree of heat can *change* the colour noticeably. My own method of patinating is to apply a basic dark tone, of either black or green, by heating the metal and brushing on the chosen solution. Then I follow

Vincent Butler at work on a small bronze cast

this with either a russet or a green, by spraying on the appropriate contrast, sometimes through a gas flame, until I feel happy with the result. It is always good practice to leave the cast to settle for two or three days, then, after warming it to sweat away moisture, spray on or gently brush on a minimum quantity of wax polish, buffing later to a dull glow. However, rule of thumb, guesswork and good luck are the best recipes and the only certainty about patination is uncertainty.

Mounting

All that remains now is to mount the work, if desired, on a suitable base, ready for exhibition. Bases may be of wood or stone, provided that in either case, good quality material is chosen. I have found that slate or marble are both very attractive and can be cheaper than wood. Also, they can be easily prepared in your own workshop – it only being necessary to saw and file, then polish with grit papers and steel wool to obtain a good finish. Slate should be brushed with a thin oil to darken it; marble should be left natural. Fixing a bronze cast to its base should officially be done with long bolts going right through the base, but I personally prefer to simply drill a short hole into the top and then, having attached short bronze bolts, which I make myself, to the bottom edge of the cast, I drop them in and fix with resin glue, or araldite etc. This method ensures that the cast will not work loose as is sometimes the case with bolt fixings, since they cannot be forced up too tight without risking cracking the stone. It is possible to free a resin fixing later if we ever wish to change the base, by gently tapping a chisel under it and levering the cast off.

Study of hands, bronze 1989, modelled and cast by V. Butler. Collection of Claire Lemming

Below: Bather, modelled and cast by V. Butler 1993, 12″×8″. Collection of Dr J. Jenkins, Edinburgh

7 · Casting by the Ceramic Shell Method

Ceramic shell casting, now widely practised in modern foundries, differs mainly from investment casting in the material used for the mould. In place of the traditional plaster-bound grog investment, a chemically-bound ceramic powder is used, which, being extremely hard, does not need to be built up to a bulky mass. Instead it is only thinly applied over the wax, often by spraying, and likewise for the core. Once set hard, the lightweight mould can be heated fiercely and rapidly to red heat which removes every trace of wax, so that when the metal is poured there is little danger of core gas expanding into the cast. I have only marginal knowledge of this process myself, but I believe I can perceive its advantages and some of its disadvantages over the investment mould method.

Advantages and Disadvantages

The ceramic shell, being immensely strong, is unlikely to split or crack during firing, thereby giving a more perfect cast, and equally there are no core gas problems. But, as the mould is so hard, it has to be chiselled off and the cast then sandblasted, all of which I see as rough treatment, whereas a bronze should be handled *con amore*.

The firing of the ceramic mould is rapid and very thorough which saves time and gas, but the slow drying required as each layer of ceramic is applied cancels out such saving.

The ceramic powder and its binder are very expensive and cannot be used over and over again, as is the case with investment, which is ground up and re-used with only a handful of new grog, plus plaster, being added.

Furthermore it appears that those who use the new method also make their moulds in rubber rather than in the cheap gelatine, all of which adds to the cost.

Despite my views, I feel that as time goes by, the ceramic shell method will take over from the older gelatine and investment. However, I sincerely hope that my recommended methods will survive, at least in private workshops and in art schools where costs are a priority.

8 · Modelling in Clay

It would not be appropriate, I think, to write a paper on casting methods, without at least a mention of a few ways in which one might set about the very first stage in the making of any cast, which is, of course, the initial working of the clay, as I have come across many people who wish to make sculpture, both inside art schools and out, but who feel uncertain about the most efficient method of starting off.

Working without Armatures

Most sculptors, in days gone by, started all their modelling by constructing an often complicated armature to carry the clay image. There is nothing wrong with that, except that I believe it is possible to do quite a lot of work with a much simplified armature, or even to eliminate it completely, as one would have to do in order to make work for firing. Standing figures will *always* need an armature, but figures in almost any other position can be made, either completely without, or with a much reduced armature, up to about three-quarters life size; after that, probably not. Considering the high cost of bronze foundries these days, and the often limited space available for sculptors to work in, quite small-scale figures are popular, both from the production point of view and from the exhibition and marketing angle. Excluding the standing figure, we can make almost anything in clay, provided we follow a few rules.

The initial blocking out of the image we have in mind should be done using a fairly stiff clay, it should be kept as light as possible (within reason), and it should not be hurried. This is so that it has time to dry off slightly and thereby can serve as a kind of armature itself, on top of which we can continue to work with much softer, more pliable clay, right until the completion of the work. We must at all times check that cracks do not develop as we work, and that any parts that are too heavy to hold up alone – such as the head – should have a thin wire inserted to strengthen the neck. If we intend to fire the finished piece, then the end will have to be left visible so that we can pull it out before the clay dries. When the work is finished, it must be allowed to dry to the state of leatherhardness. Then it can be carefully turned over and using a wire ended tool, the interior hollowed out as best as we are able. Finally, it should be allowed to become bone dry, and then fired to the temperature suitable for the type of clay used. In the case of a work too large to invert, it will be only possible to hollow it out by first cutting a doorway in the bulkiest part, by means of a wire cutter and scooping through it. The detached piece must then have its edges well spread with clay slip, as thick as cream, and then pressed back into position with firm determination, so that there can be no possibility of its coming away in the firing.

Armatures

In making a head in terracotta, we cannot dispense with an armature, so the process of hollowing out by slicing off a rear section along a line vertically drawn behind the ears, serves the double purpose of also freeing the work from its armature. Note that the application of clay slip is to both edges and its thorough pressing into place is of maximum importance as the heat of the kiln will undo any badly made joints; so be forewarned.

'Still Life – Winter Fruit', terracotta, by Vincent Butler, 1989

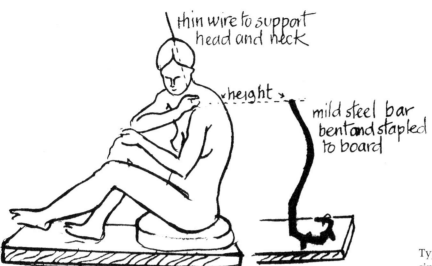

thin wire to support head and neck

height

mild steel bar bent and stapled to board

Typical seated figure on a simple armature

As with a head, works of a dimension greater than about 12in. (30cm) will need a simple armature, but it does not have to be much more than a length of iron, nailed to a board and rising to a height of about the chest, with a wire pushed down into the head and neck from above. This simple support will be freed easily enough when we cut out a 'doorway' in the back, and if we have fixed it to the board with only the bare minimum of staples, we can pull these out with pliers and extract the iron with ease.

Reclining figures, even quite large ones, need no internal armature and are hollowed out for firing either by rolling over onto one edge, or by slicing out doorways.

Animal images can present certain difficulties if they are standing upright, as even four legs will not support such a form, either during modelling or during the firing. The only way round this is to build the whole body on a pillar of clay which rises up to the belly, the head extends out from this and the legs descend without being weight-bearing. For an animal of massive volume such as an elephant, it should be possible to gradually cut away this column as the clay dries, until it is standing on its own feet, but in the case of a horse-like creature, the only possibility is to leave the column in place and maybe disguise it in some way, such as turning it into long grass or similar vegetation.

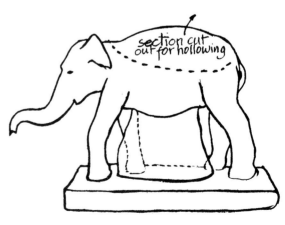

section cut out for hollowing

Animal modelled on block which might be cut away before firing

For works such as still-life groups, which will have a great mass of clay as a base with individual forms above, it is a good idea to start off by using an empty cardboard box, with thick layers of clay on all surfaces, so that it is hollow right from the beginning. The forms modelled on top of this will be hollowed out through appropriate doorways, and then, if we gently slide the whole work to the edge of our bench top and let it extend safely beyond, we will be able to reach from underneath to cut away the cardboard and trim to a fair thickness. I have known people make terracotta works by the well-established coil method (used by potters for big forms) but I find it easier to work in the methods described above.

Example of how a still life group in clay might be sectioned for hollowing out for firing

'Still Life with Grappa', terracotta, by Vincent Butler, 1993

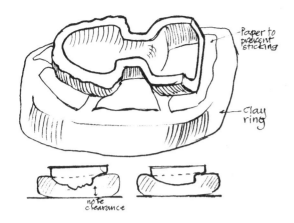

How to set up a head for hollowing out

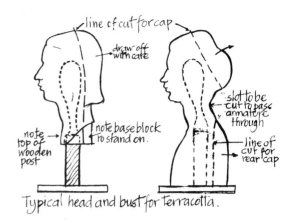

Typical head and bust for terracotta.

Methods of preparing works for hollowing out prior to firing. Clay must be leatherhard before opening up sections

Armatures for Clayworks to be Cast

Some works in clay, because of their size, as well as heads and standing figures, cannot be made without an armature. It will be useful therefore to look briefly at how we might go about constructing these. Some can be self supporting with no external parts; others will have an outside iron that will carry all the weight and render the armature more flexible at the same time. An armature that is completely internal will not differ from that required where we wish to construct a work directly in plaster. It will be of mild steel rods, preferably welded together, and will have to be very accurate to avoid unwelcome intrusion through the surface modelling. In this sense it is the less preferable of the two, and I would always recommend the external type.

Standing Figures

The exception is the case of a standing figure not taller than about 12in. (30cm), where I would use one iron only, bent carefully, through the standing leg and stapled to the baseboard. This should rise to chest height only; the other leg will be without any metal. The head and neck will have the usual thin wire inserted from above. The advantage of this method is that we have greater accuracy with only one iron to think about, and of course we do not have to

split our mould at the entry point of the external support when casting.

A standing figure more than 12in. (30cm) high will need a very strong armature constructed on an external 'L' iron. The metal for the armature itself will be a mild steel bar and will vary in thickness from ¼in. (6mm) up to ¾in. (2cm) according to the size of the work. It is most important to calculate the proportions of the figure to ensure that the back iron enters in the lumbar region and not below. The full weight of the clay will be taken by the 'L' iron, so it is not necessary for the leg metals to touch the baseboard. They should just clear the base, which means that we will be able to shift them about if we wish.

The separate parts of the armature should be tied together with binding wire. It is not a good idea to weld them as this only makes it more difficult to extract the armature from the inside of the mould later. Also, the 'L' iron should be bolted to the baseboard with the nuts *above*, so that it is possible to detach it and remove it from the mould while still upright. This will hardly be necessary for a small work, but for a life-sized figure it can be very useful indeed. Note also that a large figure should be modelled on a double baseboard, with heavy wooden spacers, so that any warping due to dampness and the great weight will not affect the free running of the wheels below.

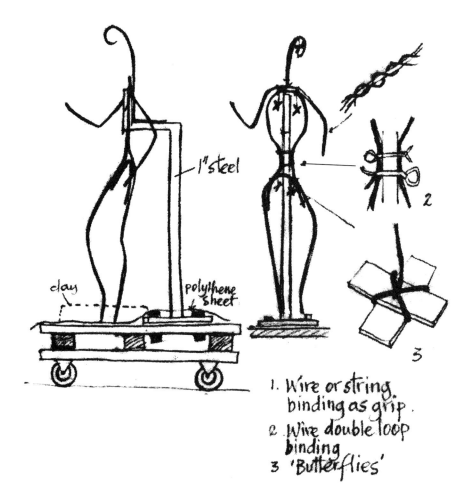

1" steel

clay

polythene sheet

1. Wire or string binding as grip.
2. Wire double loop binding
3. 'Butterflies'

2

3

Typical armature for a life-sized figure

3/16th" m.s. bar on single vertical pole

split wooden bench.

free wire

thin wire binding down to calf.

small scale standing figure on ¼" m.s.

Life-sized seated figure armature

Sitting Figures

Sitting figures will not require an external 'L' iron, as it is generally possible to fix our metals to a single pole of strong steel rising up to the waist level through the pelvis. In a large sitting figure, if we do not want to have a large mass of clay under the figure, we might construct a simple bench form, in wood, in two parts, one to the front and one to the back, meeting at the upright metal pole. This will then be drawn out while casting. In all cases, the metals should be bound with thin wire, or with string, to give a good grip to the clay, and we should tie so-called 'butterflies' to the armature at places where the clay will be at its most massive. These are bits of wood lath tied horizontally with wire on which the clay will rest.

One final point to note with a large work – I have observed students making big figures right down on the baseboard or at any rate with only the merest clay base. I think this is unwise, and would always have a good thickness of clay below the feet of my figure. We can always cast with less if we wish, but if we have not made our calculations of proportion accurate enough, we might find that we are not able to drop down a little if we need to, unless the underlying clay is really thick.

Firing Terracotta Works

These days it should not be much of a problem to get access to a local potter or ceramic studio for the firing of one's work, rather than buying a kiln for one's own studio. However, a few words of caution. Ceramists normally fire their products at a fairly fast rate, and are able to do so because they will be working with thin sections, and their clay will probably have been wedged beforehand (that is kneaded hard to remove air), whereas a modelled work will be neither of these. (Even if we do go to the trouble of wedging we only re-introduce air by the very action of modelling.) Therefore, we must absolutely ensure that we have a long, slow firing, especially at the start. I would

recommend not more than 100°C in the first day. Ceramists often resist such slow firing, and when they burst work for us they lose no time in condemning our naïveté in using unwedged, dirty or unsuitable clay. All I can say is that in thirty years of teaching I must have fired, who knows, thousands of students' works, all of them modelled in the 'wrong' clay, unwedged and often enough a bit too thick in section, and can only recall the total loss of *one* piece. I have experienced cracks and limited bursting, of maybe a leg, a back, an arm, but I have always been able to repair such damage afterwards with resin glue mixed with grog, or even with plaster where I was prepared to colour the work later, but even then I am speaking of about two per cent or less. However, I must stress that we can only expect success with our average sculptor's modelling clay if we follow the three basic rules mentioned above:

1. Hollow out as much as possible,
2. dry out totally and completely, and
3. fire dead slow.

There arc clays available, such as for example, 'Crank Craft', whose grog content is so high that it will resist poor hollowing out and fast firing, but I personally find such gritty material unpleasant to model with on a small scale and have always used finer, smoother clays, such as 'Potclay's' stoneware grey, or their red terracotta clay, both of which are very plastic and sensitive, while 'Crank' is 'short' and only really good for very large-scale work.

Glazing

I am often asked by students about techniques of glazing fired works, but I am unable to advise, as I have no knowledge of glazes such as ceramists would use, and I doubt if it is so important for sculptors to use coloured glazes. I have, however, on occasion, made a work in a red body, allowed it to dry out and then coated it, by spraying or splashing, with a grey clay slip, dried again and then cut back by discreet rubbing with wire wool, resulting in, after firing, a dark background enriched by pale tones in the hollows. On other occasions, when I have found the result of my firing to be unsatisfactory, either due to the oxidising atmosphere of the electric kiln which produces a pallid, colourless surface, or because it has been necessary to fill cracks or other blemishes on the surface, I have toned the work by adding washes of oil colour well diluted with turps. If this is done lightly and repeatedly, perhaps alternating the colour between, say, Vandyke brown, burnt sienna and earth red, it is possible to build up a very attractive 'glaze' without totally changing the fact that it is a terracotta.

I acknowledge the fact that there will be some purists who see such touching up as slightly dishonest, but then I console myself by remembering that most antique statuary, whether bronze or marble, or indeed wood, had patching or similar repair work to the surface (note Donatello's bronze David for example), which was later disguised under a layer of patina of one kind or another. It is a well-known fact that Roman marble carvers frequently filled in surface blemishes on their work with a mixture of marble dust and beeswax. Discriminating clients who were looking for perfect products, and had the means to pay extra for them, would demand statues *Sine Cera*, that is without wax, from which we derive our modern word 'sincere'. In my book, sincerity is more to do with the poetic content of the work than with its physical perfection, although, naturally, one strives all one's life to improve one's craft. These days it is common practice to touch up surface defects with a mixture of resin glue and whatever is the base material, be it marble, bronze or wood, ground to a fine powder. This adheres well and is harder than beeswax, but we do not yet know if it will last as long.

9 · General Information about Casting Metals for Sculpture

Bronze is an alloy of copper and tin, and these two metals apparently occur together in the natural ore. Ancient bronze statues were therefore cast with the two metals in proportion of about 90% copper and 10% tin. Modern bronzes are usually an alloy of approximately 85% copper, 5% tin, 5% zinc and 5% lead, which in the trade is known as leaded gun metal. In statuary, it is the copper which gives the rich patination. Low copper alloys such as one often finds in 'bronzes' offered for sale in Mediterranean countries and in Asia, do not lend themselves to good patination and are often very thin, as the high zinc content (or lead) means that the metal flows like water, and fine details are easily obtained thereby.

In Victorian times a popular metal for casting statues was known as Britannia Metal. I do not know its composition but it was whitish in colour and was certainly not bronze. In the Far East it was popular to cast in an alloy of 50/50 copper and lead, giving a blackish metal. All of the abovementioned concoctions are easily breakable, have low melting points (try welding one and you will see it run away like quicksilver), and their 'bronze' colour will not be a true patina but will be paint or lacquer. On the other hand, the traditional temple bronzes made in India and perhaps other countries where Hindu cults exist, were cast with an added quantity of gold and silver as a sign of respect for the deity. Interestingly also, it was

habitual to leave the core inside the cast, or alternatively to fill it with sacred texts, because it was considered unfitting for a God to be hollow.

In recent years it has been common to find galleries offering so called 'cold cast' bronzes for sale, a contradiction in terms if ever there was one, as such products are made of resin with bronze powder and are in fact, plastic.

Brass, being a mixture of 60% copper and 40% zinc, is more acceptable as a 'true' metal for casting, but its lower copper content makes patination difficult. It is also more unpleasant to work with as it fumes fiercely with zinc oxide during melting and it is also harder to chase later, having no tin in the composition to render it malleable. However, it has been widely used for sculpture. For example, the well-known Benin and Ife bronzes have been analysed to be nearer to brass than bronze, and certainly the local bronze workers I visited in West Africa were using the brass scrap from derelict lorry gearboxes for their castings.

Lead, being the cheapest of casting metals, was very popular in the eighteenth century for the production of copies or versions of famous Italian Renaissance or Baroque sculpture, and many British country houses have such pieces in their gardens. Unfortunately, however, its lifespan is short and after a century or so it begins to collapse and fall apart. A fine example of lead statuary is the equestrian Charles II in

Parliament Square in Edinburgh, which has survived well. It was among the earliest of lead castings produced in Britain, although it was in sorry condition by the middle of this century and was extensively restored by Morris Singer in the 1970s.

Aluminium is harder than lead and some sculptors have made use of it; for example, Alfred Gilbert's Eros in Piccadilly is an aluminium cast. It too was badly in need of restoration by the mid-1980s and was repaired by Hendersons of Edinburgh, under the direction of George Mancini. As will be clear from the contents of this book, the costs in casting are incurred because of the complex operations in the moulding and finishing, and therefore, although brass, lead and aluminium cost less than bronze, there is little real saving in using such 'inferior' metals and bronze, or gun metal, as we prefer to call it in the trade, remains the best and most prestigious metal for modelled sculpture.

Parvati, consort of Siva,
Chola bronze,
12th century,
Thanjavur Museum

10 · George Mancini, Bronze Caster par excellence

Many of the techniques described in this book were acquired during the years I had the privilege of working with the late George Mancini, bronze caster par excellence, whom I assisted in running a casting course at the College of Art in Edinburgh in the 1980s, after he had retired from his own foundry in Fountainbridge. Mancini, who liked to be called by his surname, had his early training with his father in London, later transferring to Cheltenham and eventually settling in Scotland just before the war. He ran his foundry single handedly and had never had any teaching contact with the Art School previously. Therefore I can consider myself to be his first apprentice, and although I had done a little casting beforehand, I really learned all I know from him.

Despite his origins, Mancini had never been to Italy but he still recalled some of the good humoured banter heard in his father's foundry, as for example, just as we were about to pour the metal, he would pretend to dip a finger into the glowing crucible, then tasting it pensively, he would look up at me and say in a thick Roman accent, 'Vincenzo, hai dimenticato il sale ancora' (you forgot the salt again), or some equally dotty remark. Casting with Mancini was always a memorable event, revealing not only his great skills and his immense care and attention at all stages of the work, but also his wry humour which provided that necessary yeast to the often leaden dough of art school life.

The following pages contain a description of Mancini's method of casting a life-sized figure from the plaster through the wax stage to the bronze.

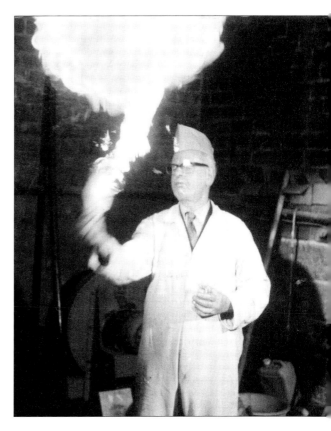

George Mancini playing with fire

George Mancini's Method of Making a Mould for a Wax of a Life-sized Figure in Plaster

1. Lie figure on back on two cushions and two ropes.
2. Mark a waist line with pencil or shellacked string.
3. Surround with bricks or wood blocks and overlay with plaster collar, shellac. Place board to base.

4. Shellac figure and give light coat of oil or cover with polyfilm. Clay up entire front making seam at belt, add grips, sprues and air vents.

5. Case up front in three sections, i.e. legs, belt and bust with cradle clearing belt section.

6. Rope up and turn right over to rest on cradle.

7. Clay up back in three or four sections, and make corresponding cases.

8. Hammer in dogs and turn back on to cushions.

9. Strip clay from leg section, shellac case, oil and then pour gelatine.

10. Repeat for belt and head section, but pour gelatine as one.

11. Turn over and make gelatine on back section 1.

12. Make next sections in turn, but last two together.

13. Turn over again and remove cases and gelatines from front sections.

14. Cut belt section free, replace, treat all sections with alum and replace in cases, knocking nails into sprues to hold gelatines in position.

15. Repeat for back.

16. Paint and paste wax to all sections up to ¼in. (6mm) thick.

17. Close upper and lower moulds separately and fill seams. Make wax fillets around edges of waist sections at joint.

18. Make wax sleeve for belt section, remove from case and register into lower half (oil to avoid sticking), pressing sleeve well all around to ensure accurate joint. Then remove from its gelatine and place it edge to edge against top section, hot sealing into place.

19. Stand lower mould upright, place reinforcing irons loose inside legs then fill with core, solid in legs and then hollow in waist, line at top with chicken netting.

20. Remove case(s) and gelatine from lower half, touch up seams where required. **Note**, in a heavy figure it is advisable at this point to cut out a square of wax from the base between the feet, so that the base core will be in contact with the investment, otherwise it might close up under its own weight. Cast this square apart, and fix to bronze later.

21. Core up bust section, head and neck solid and bust hollow.

22. Remove cases and gelatines, touch up seams.

23. Knock in core nails, if not done, through wax before adding core, then gate up each half.

24. Invest in usual way, burn out moulds and pour bronze.

25. After fettling it should be easy to slip belt sleeve down into place in waist. If the fit is not perfect, the following procedure will tighten any slackness. Whitewash joint and position. On removal again any tight spots will show, file these down and repeat until good fit is obtained.

26. Joining two sections together.

   a. Drill four holes in upper edge of leg section.
   b. Fit to bust section and mark through to sleeve.
   c. Drill these marks out ⅛in. (3mm) lower.
   d. Fit sections together and knock 'drifts' (tapered bolts) through holes. These will force the two sections to fit tightly together. Drill four new holes and plug with bronze screws. Remove drifts and plug likewise.

27. Complete all fettling and chasing. Patinate as desired.

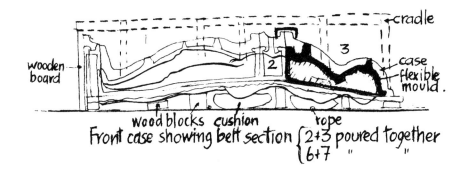

wooden board

cradle

3

2

case flexible mould.

wood blocks   cushion   rope

Front case showing belt section { 2+3 poured together
                                  6+7   "   "

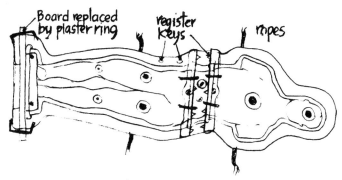

Board replaced by plaster ring

register keys

ropes

Note For simplicity the arms have been excluded
they would be cast separately and jointed later

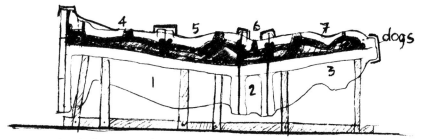

4   5   6   7   dogs

1   2   3

Mould turned onto cradle and back made in 4 or 5 parts

Mancini's method of making a mould of a life-sized figure

George Mancini's Method of Making a Roman Joint

Example: an arm

1. Mark position on horizontal seam for register, with vertical lines, in two places.
2. Make case and gelatine of arm and paint wax as usual.
3. With wax still in case, cut out a sleeve about 1in. (2.5cm) deep and add fillet to lower edge.
4. Add lug all around inside (or part way where arm is close to body), check in mould for possible warping.
5. Position onto shoulder, using registers and hot join.
6. Cast body and arm into bronze.
7. After fettling, sleeve should slide exactly inside arm.
8. Drill offset holes and tighten in place with drifts, thread and plug in usual way, hammer out fillet and chase.

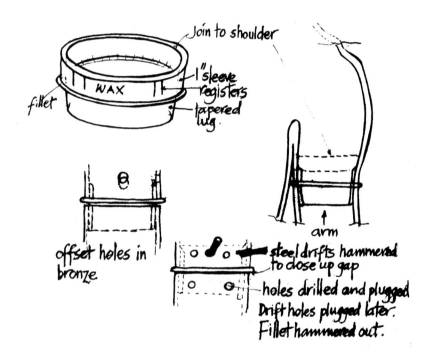

Mancini's Roman joint

11 · Tools

I have frequently been asked what kind of tools are necessary for sculpture and my reply to this has usually been – 'very few'. For modelling I depend more on my ten fingers than on anything else, although quite clearly some kind of cutting tool, such as an old kitchen knife, is required from time to time.

A slightly better instrument than a knife would be a metal plasterer's spatula, obtainable from any good artist's materials supplier and I would recommend the type with a curved leaf blade at one end as this is very useful for scraping the surfaces of materials such as plaster or wax. For hollowing out a clay in preparation for firing, a ring-ended tool is necessary but a twist of coat hanger wire will serve equally well.

For chipping out a plaster cast, an old and blunt flat chisel is all that is required and an ordinary half pound hammer. I personally use a lead hammer, which I made myself for this purpose and also for carving both stone and wood as its great advantage is that it is *silent* and being soft it does not easily slip and hit your thumb!

Obviously, for chasing bronzes one needs a few good engineer's chisels as well as various files, taps and dies, and almost certainly a power drill and grinder, but these can be obtained a few at a time and need not cost you an arm and a leg.

For carving I use surprisingly few tools. For stone I have a couple of points and two or three flat chisels. Tungsten-tipped chisels are the best, but steel ones will do fine if you are prepared to re-grind them regularly. For wood I have three gouges, 2", 1½" and 1" and I find these to be all that is required.

For modelling in clay up to about 50 kilos in weight, it is useful to have a professional modelling stand, but as there are very few companies producing such items, they are extremely expensive and it is perfectly possible to make use of an old packing case, or something similar. If you wish to model something of greater weight and volume, then you will have to use a baseboard with wheels.

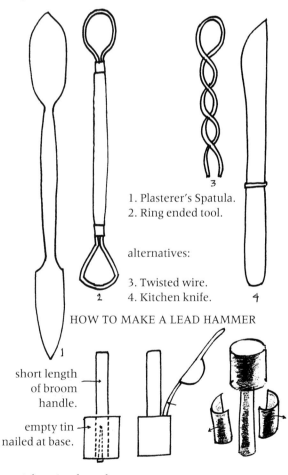

1. Plasterer's Spatula.
2. Ring ended tool.

alternatives:

3. Twisted wire.
4. Kitchen knife.

HOW TO MAKE A LEAD HAMMER

short length of broom handle.

empty tin nailed at base.

A few simple tools

'Heritage and Hope', a life-sized bronze group, by Vincent Butler for Atlas Square, Springburn, Glasgow, 1989.
Cast by Burleighfield Foundry, High Wycombe

12 · The Making of 'Heritage and Hope: Springburn 1989'

Bronze group by Vincent Butler, RSA, for Atlas Square, Springburn, Glasgow.

'... depicting a foundryman in pre-war working clothes and a young girl in a dancing/skipping posture, both figures appearing to move in a forward direction. The mood of the statue is light-hearted and optimistic as it is a metaphor both for the industrial past of Springburn, represented by the man, and for the future, in the figure of the young girl in modern clothing, spreading her arms out towards a new world.'

1. Maquette

Having received the brief from the planning department, suggesting the subject matter, the sculptor prepared a maquette or sketch indicating how he proposed to interpret the theme. This was modelled in wax and cast in bronze by the sculptor himself.

2. Scale Model

The next stage was to make a scale model in clay which was then cast into plaster, so that problems of composition, pose, movement etc. could be solved. For this living models were used, and the figures modelled nude, so that the proper articulation of the limbs could be determined.

Right
Maquette or sketch of proposed statue, modelled in wax and cast into bronze by the sculptor.

3. The Figures in Clay

The next stage began by constructing two metal armatures, mounted on separate baseboards with wheels. These were carefully proportioned from measurements taken from the living models. Then, each figure was modelled, in clay, separately, using nude models. This method ensures that the finished figures will have the appearance of possessing real, solid bodies beneath the clothing, and will not look like merely hollow frames draped in cloth, as on a scarecrow. Obviously certain surface details are omitted if the figures are left in an 'unfinished' state, but the main mass of muscles, bones etc. are all there, and of course those parts not covered by clothes are taken to a high degree of finish (faces, arms, hands etc.). Subsequently, the clothing was added to the figures, using, in part, real cloth soaked in wet clay, and in part solid clay modelled to represent the clothing.

Scale model of proposed statue. Modelled in clay and cast into plaster. Figures modelled nude; final composition determined at this time.

82

The full-sized figure of the man, modelled nude (an early stage in the work)

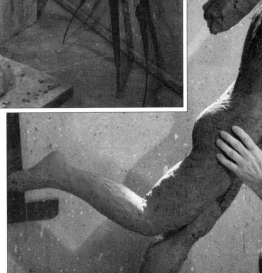

The sculptor at work on the full-sized figure of the girl.

4. Casting the Figures into Plaster

Having taken the modelling to a satisfactory degree of completion, the sculptor then had the task of converting the clay into a permanent material – in this case, plaster of paris. The means used for this was casting by the so-called waste mould method, which meant that the mould gave only one cast and the original was destroyed in the process. The first step in this was to lay bands of clay vertically and horizontally along predetermined lines of division on each figure. Then the front 'half' of each figure was coated about 1in. (2.5cm) thick with casting plaster, suitably reinforced with steel bar and a wooden supporting frame or 'cradle'. The clay bands were then removed and the resulting seams greased. Finally, the rear 'half' of each figure was coated, but this time not as one single section but in numerous pieces that were built on one by one.

Having thus created the mould, the sections were prised off and the clay removed from the inside, until a hollow shell was achieved. This was then washed, coated with a separator – soft soap in this case – and reassembled. Strong internal reinforcements were set into the mould, and section by section the separate pieces were clamped into place and liquid plaster poured into the hollow, filling the legs solid and the upper half about 2in. (5cm) thick. Once this was done, the sculptor began immediately to remove the mould, by chipping it away with a hammer and chisel. This was a painstaking task but slowly the figure underneath re-emerged.

Naturally there was a great deal of adjustment necessary at this stage and considerable reworking of the surface took place. Also in this particular piece, the man's arms (which were removed from the clay and moulded separately) had to be replaced – using 'Roman joints' (mortice and tenon); likewise for the girl's hands and her pony-tail hair. In addition, the two figures had to be matched together so that their bases met up level and square, and the edges jointed so that the two figures could separate for transport. Having done all this the sculptor added signature and date to the base.

These first stages took the sculptor in all about 12 weeks effort, working every day for about 10–12 hours.

Opposite
The male figure, near completion in clay, with the clothing added; using part real cloth and part modelled

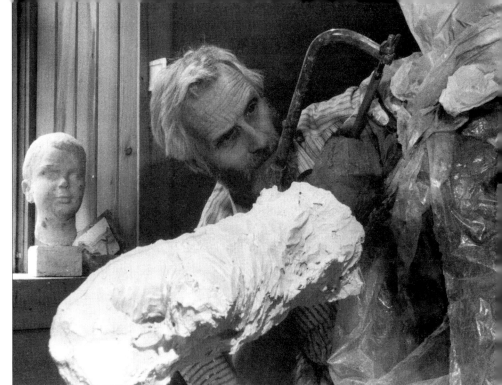

The arms of the male figure, having been moulded, are sawn off completely, and plaster casts are subsequently made.

The male figure being prepared for casting. The photograph shows the clay walls or bands that will separate the mould into 'halves'. The front will have three pieces and there will be seven at the back.

86

Left
The completed moulds are cracked open by means of wedges driven into the seams which force the sections apart

Below
The mould of the girl having its internal reinforcement fixed in place

Left
The male figure. The steel reinforcing bars being fixed inside the mould with plaster

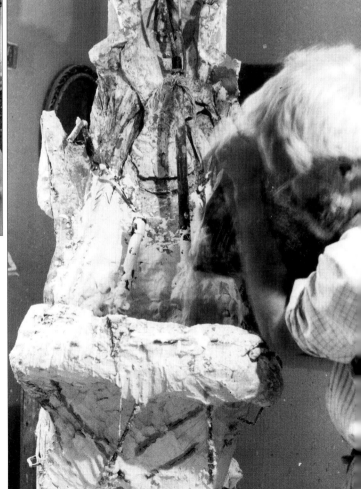

Right
The lower half of the mould is now in place and the sculptor is pouring plaster inside to fill the legs. The cast will be solid to the hips and the whole upper part will be hollow

Right and Below
The completed cast is now removed from its mould by means of a hammer and chisel. This means that only one cast may be produced from the mould

The finished casts being assembled. The arms are 'Roman jointed' or morticed into place so that they may be removed for transport to the foundry, and to facilitate the bronze casting.

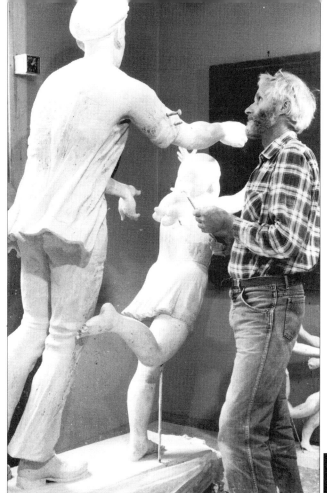

Left
The sculptor with the finished plaster cast

Below
Lynsay Clark, who posed for the young girl

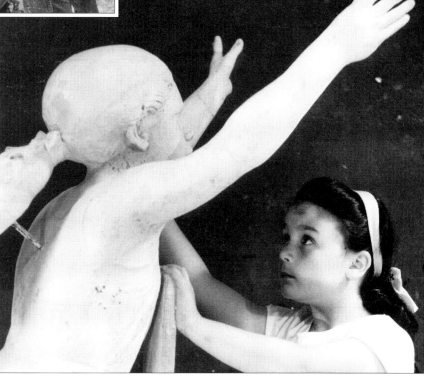

5. Casting the Group into Bronze

As soon as the group was dried out thoroughly, it was crated and sent by road to Buckinghamshire for casting. The foundry selected for this was Burleighfield of High Wycombe, and they chose a combination of two methods for this, the 'lost wax' method for the man's arms and the girl's head and hands, and the sand casting method for all the rest.

The lost wax technique meant that another mould had to be made of each item to be cast, using a rubber mould in a plaster shell. From these flexible moulds hollow wax casts were made. This job is very specialised and great care had to be used to ensure a perfect reproduction was produced, matching exactly the original. These waxes were then coated, inside and out, with a refractory material – in this case siliminite – to form moulds. These were fired in a kiln to about 1000°C, which burnt away all the wax, and liquid bronze was then poured in through appropriate channels or openings. Once cooled, the moulds were broken apart, revealing the casts, ready for trimming and cleaning.

Meanwhile, the rest of the group, the bodies and legs and bases, were prepared for sand casting. Again, this is a highly skilled task that involved the figures being laid horizontally in a frame and special sand packed to a halfway mark. The figure was then lifted out leaving its impression in the sand, like a footprint on a beach. The process was repeated for the other half of the figure. (In practice there were more than two 'halves' in order to account for the deep modelling or undercutting.) The completed mould was hardened by the addition of CO_2 gas and finally a 'core' or inside figure had to be made to fit in this interior, in order to make a hollow bronze about ¼in. (6mm) thick.

Once the core was in place, the mould was locked together and molten bronze poured in through appropriate channels. When the metal had cooled, the moulds were broken open and the cast removed for trimming and cleaning. Finally, the separate parts were reassembled, pinned and welded together and the bronze and the bases jointed to make the complete group.

Lastly the bronze was 'patinated' or coloured. This meant that a chemical reagent was brushed onto the surface to darken it and sealed in place with hot beeswax, thus giving the golden brown lustre we see on the finished product. This part of the work took a further 12 weeks.

The stone plinth was made by Stewart McGlashan of Shotts and the lettered panel designed and cut in plaster by the sculptor and cast into bronze by Laing's foundry in Edinburgh.

'Bathers', 1996, modelled and cast by Vincent Butler. 10" high

'Still life with Violin'. Maquette for proposed bronze for the Royal Concert Hall, Glasgow, 1989. 3′ 6″ high. Modelled by V. Butler. Cast by Art Bronze Foundry, Fulham.

List of Suppliers

Plaster

British Gypsum Ltd
Jericho Works
Bowbridge Road
Newark, Notts. NG24 3BZ, UK
01636-703351

Cookson Ceramics Ltd
Uttoxeter Road
Meir, Stoke-on-Trent ST3 7XW, UK
01782-599111

Laguna Clay Company
14400 Lomitas Avenue
City of Industry, CA91746, USA
800-452-4862

Whitfields Minerals Ltd
Whitfield House
10 Water Street
Newcastle-under-Lyme,
Staffordshire ST5 1HP, UK
01782-711155

Clays

Axner Pottery Supply
PO Box 621484
Oviedo, FL 32762 USA
407-365-7057

Bath Potters' Supplies
2 Dorset Close,
East Twerton, Bath BA2 3RF, UK
01225-337046

Briar Wheels and Supplies Ltd
Whitsbury Road
Fordingbridge, Hampshire SP6 1NQ, UK
01425-652991

Potclays
Brickkiln Lane
Etruria, Stoke-on-Trent ST4 7BP, UK
01782-219816

Potterycrafts Ltd/Reward Clayglaze
Campbell Road
Stoke-on-Trent ST4 4ET, UK
01782-745000

Tucker's Pottery Supplies
15 West Pearce Street
Richmond Hill, Ontario L4B 1H6, Canada
905-889-7705

Other moulding products

Alec Tiranti
27 Warren Street
London W1P 5DG
0171-636-8565

Kingfisher Ceramics Service
Bycors Road
Heathcote Works
Burselm, Stoke-on-Trent ST6 4EQ, UK
01782-575254

J. W. Ratcliffe & Sons
Rope Works
Shelton New Road
Stoke-on-Trent ST4 6DJ, UK
01782-611321

Index

animals 23–4
armatures 65, 67, 69, 70

burn-out kiln 56
brass shims 13
bronze casting 45–64

case moulds 28, 29, 32, 34–7
casting
    bronze 45–64
    ceramic shell method of 64
    in cement 41–2
    in glass fibre resin 43–4
    small details 15, 16
cement 38–42
clay, modelling in 65–72
colouring casts 25
core vents 52, 60
cores 49, 50
cradles 15, 18

detailed work 15–16
dog clamps 13

figures 17–22, 69–71, 75–8

gating systems 53, 58–60
gelatine 27–31, 32, 34–5
glass fibre reinforced resin 43–4
glazing 71–2
grog 50

heads 12–14, 33–5
'Heritage and Hope: Springburn 1989' 81–92

jute scrim 16, 18, 20, 27

kilns, burn-out 56

lost wax process 45–64
ludo 50, 55

Mancini, G. 8, 75–8
metals for casting 73–4
micro-crystalline wax 45
modelling
    in clay 65–72
    in plaster and cement 38–40
moulds 10–26
    gelatine 27–31
    mother 11, 17, 22
    piece 27
    repairs to 13
    waste 45–6
    wax 16
M.S. reinforcing bars 11, 20

patination 63
plaster
    modelling in 28–40
    repairs to 13
    types 25
    use of 25

relief work 15–17
resin, casting in glass fibre reinforced 43–4
rosin 48
rubber 31–3
    cold cast 36–7

seam walls 11, 22
separators 24–5, 44

terracotta 68, 69, 71
tools 79

vinyl 31–3

wax moulds 16, 45–6, 75–8